EVALUATING JUVENILE JUSTICE

Volume 29
SAGE RESEARCH PROGRESS SERIES IN CRIMINOLOGY

SAGE RESEARCH PROGRESS SERIES IN CRIMINOLOGY

Published in Cooperation with the American Society of Criminology

Series Editor: **MICHAEL R. GOTTFREDSON,** *State University of New York at Albany*

Founding Series Editor: **JAMES A. INCIARDI,** *University of Delaware*

VOLUMES IN THIS SERIES (editor / title)

1. ROBERT F. MEIER / Theory in Criminology
2. THEODORE N. FERDINAND / Juvenile Delinquency
3. C. RONALD HUFF / Contemporary Corrections
4. ALVIN W. COHN / Criminal Justice Planning and Development
5. JAMES A. INCIARDI, ANNE E. POTTIEGER / Violent Crime
6. MARVIN D. KROHN, RONALD L. AKERS / Crime, Law, and Sanctions
7. JOHN P. CONRAD / The Evolution of Criminal Justice
8. CHARLES WELLFORD / Quantitative Studies in Criminology
9. MARGARET EVANS / Discretion and Control
10. C. R. JEFFERY / Biology and Crime
11. WILLIAM H. PARSONAGE / Perspectives on Victimology
12. DAVID M. PETERSEN / Police Work
13. PAUL J. BRANTINGHAM, JACK M. KRESS / Structure, Law, and Power
14. PATRICIA L. BRANTINGHAM, TIM G. BLOMBERG / Courts and Diversion
15. EDWARD SAGARIN / Taboos in Criminology
16. BARBARA RAFFEL PRICE / Criminal Justice Research
17. ALVIN W. COHN, BENJAMIN WARD / Improving Management in Criminal Justice
18. TRAVIS HIRSCHI, MICHAEL GOTTFREDSON / Understanding Crime
19. RONALD ROESCH, RAYMOND R. CORRADO / Evaluation and Criminal Justice Policy
20. JAMES J. FYFE / Contemporary Issues in Law Enforcement
21. MARGUERITE Q. WARREN / Comparing Male and Female Offenders
22. GARY F. JENSEN / Sociology of Delinquency
23. SIMON HAKIM, GEORGE F. RENGERT / Crime Spillover
24. JOHN HAGAN / Quantitative Criminology
25. VICTORIA L. SWIGERT / Law and the Legal Process
26. MERRY MORASH / Implementing Criminal Justice Policies
27. HAROLD E. PEPINSKY / Rethinking Criminology
28. JOHN HAGAN / Deterrence Reconsidered
29. JAMES R. KLUEGEL / Evaluating Juvenile Justice
30. GORDON P. WALDO / Career Criminals
31. ISRAEL L. BARAK-GLANTZ, ELMER H. JOHNSON / Comparative Criminology
32. GORDON P. WALDO / Measurement Issues in Criminal Justice

SAGE RESEARCH PROGRESS SERIES IN CRIMINOLOGY
VOLUME 29

EVALUATING JUVENILE JUSTICE

EDITED BY
JAMES R. KLUEGEL

Published in cooperation with the
AMERICAN SOCIETY OF CRIMINOLOGY

SAGE PUBLICATIONS
Beverly Hills / London / New Delhi

Copyright © 1983 by Sage Publications, Inc.

All rights reserved. No part of this book may be reproduced or utilized in any form or by any means, electronic or mechanical, including photo-copying, recording, or by any information storage and retrieval system, without permission in writing from the publisher.

For information address:

SAGE Publications, Inc.
275 South Beverly Drive
Beverly Hills, California 90212

SAGE Publications India Pvt. Ltd.
C-236 Defence Colony
New Delhi 110 024, India

SAGE Publications Ltd
28 Banner Street
London EC1Y 8QE, England

Printed in the United States of America

Library of Congress Cataloging in Publication Data

Main entry under title:

Evaluating juvenile justice.

   (Sage research progress series in criminology ; v. 29)
   "Published in cooperation with the American Society of Criminology."
   Bibliography: p.
   1. Juvenile justice, Administration of—United States—
Evaluation—Addresses, essays, lectures. I. Kluegel,
James R. II. Series.
HV9104.E94   1983   364.3'6'0973   83-13691
ISBN 0-8039-2116-0

FIRST PRINTING

843332

LIBRARY
ALMA COLLEGE
ALMA, MICHIGAN

CONTENTS

LIBRARY
ALMA COLLEGE
ALMA, MICHIGAN

EVALUATING JUVENILE JUSTICE

James R. Kluegel

University of Illinois at Urbana Champaign

CONTEMPORARY JUVENILE JUSTICE
Responding to Public Mandates for Change

Criminology, as other social science disciplines, responded enthusiastically to the invitation offered as part of the "Great Society" program of the 1960s to aid in the solution of social problems. As scholars whose subject of study is among the problems of most public concern, we have been able to command a large share of the governmental funds allocated to research on ameliorating social problems. As a result of the inflow of funds criminology and criminal justice have been "growth industries" in the last two decades. Even in the late 1970s, when the fortunes of other areas of study in the social sciences were waning somewhat, criminology maintained its vitality as an area of research funding. Indicatively in the 1970s researchers in criminology were able to acquire funds io carry out several large field experiments to evaluate proposed new and ongoing policies and practices for crime reduction, such as the Texas and Georgia experiments in providing released felons with transitional unemployment payments to reduce recidivism (Rossi et al., 1980).

In other circumstances this might be a time for the discipline to engage in self-congratulation. Until recently we seemed to have gained some recognition that we can make important contributions to criminal justice practice both as initiators and evaluators of policy. Further, few would deny the claim that the sophistication and quality of research on issues of criminal justice have markedly improved in the last two decades as scholars from several social science diciplines have been attracted to research in the area by the challenge policy-relevant research presents and by the resources available to carry it out. Instead of self-congratulation, however, the discipline seems to be currently engaged in much more self-criticism and self-defense. Through numerous publications in the last several years policy researchers have engaged in a wide-ranging dialogue on such topics as whether or not treatment programs have any benefit (Fishman, 1977; Gendrau and Ross, 1981; Gottfredson, 1979, 1982; Martinson, 1974; Palmer, 1975; Roesch and Corrado, 1979; Wilson, 1975) and the worth of evaluation research itself (Corrado, 1981; Hackler, 1978, 1979; Roesch and Corrado, 1981).

One reason for this dialogue is, of course, that the social reform and treatment orientations that prevail among policy advocates have been the subject of vigorous attack by some scholars, politicians, and, at least indirectly, public opinion (Jensen 1981). The strong public and political sentiment for the thesis that social reforms and treatment programs for reducing crime have failed has been accompanied by public and political demands for new policy. Seemingly under the assumption that since social reform and treatment have failed, deterrence must work, or by the virtue of a desperate desire to try something "new" (at least "new" in contrast to the assumed liberal orientation of the recent past) much sentiment has been generated for deterrence or for "getting tough on criminals." Demands for such change have been made at all levels of criminal justice, including the area of focus in this volume—juvenile justice.

The chapters presented in this volume share the theme of evaluating publicly mandated change in juvenile justice practices. The issues discussed and the programs evaluated in these chapters reflect the seemingly abrupt shift in ideological emphasis that characterized the decade of the 1970s—from the liberal emphasis on programs to divert certain youths from juvenile court processing to the conservative emphasis on identifying serious or career delinquents for special treatment and, in many cases, more adult-like adjudication and dispositions. Collectivly, these chapters present one response to public and political demands for change in juvenile justice practice: Treat all such mandates equally by subjecting them to the same type of scholarly scrutiny of their potential benefits and drawbacks; by subjecting proposed new policies to experimentation; and by evaluating the results of such experiments accordingly to professional standards, with at least the collective effort to maintain professional detachment from the implications of research results. In many respects the response by policy researchers in juvenile justice has followed the prescriptions for establishing an experimenting society (Campbell, 1969).

At present, however, there seems to be a suspicion that this means of response to publicly mandated change may be denied, all or in part, to policy researchers in juvenile justice and criminal justice more broadly. This suspicion is implicit or explicit in the literature cited earlier that defends evaluation research from the multiple sources of recent attack. Further, there is some fear that even if the prevailing belief that past policy research has failed to produce useful results does not lead to its end altogether, it may so constrict inquiry as to make it frustrating and perhaps unproductive exercise. This sentiment is expressed implicitly in the article by Saul and Davidson in this volume. They conclude that, as currently operated, juvenile diversion programs serve to widen the net of social control by involving juveniles who otherwise would be informally handled and released. Yet, they suspect that if diversion programs would operate to avoid referral of cases not originally targeted for diversion, they may be beneficial. This is, of course, in part a call for the kind of follow-up inquiry that often results from inital research on policy. But as Saul and Davidson lament, federal funds for further research on diversion are now disappearing, and thus the prospects for such follow-up research appear bleak.

In the recent past we have had to think little about how to respond to public mandates for change in juvenile justice practice, since both public attitudes and political leadership supported the emphasis on social reform and treatment that prevailed among advocates. Now it appears that we must give this issue more careful thought. Put directly, how does policy research on juvenile justice avoid becoming the baby thrown out with the bath water? In the remainder of this chapter I will discuss two lines of response to the current political and public demands for a change that, in my view, may be benificial.

SUGGESTED RESPONSES TO THE NEW MANDATES

"Stay the Course"

The first line of response, I suggest, should be to keep responding to requests to initiate and evaluate new juvenile justice programs when the opportunity is presented. To borrow a phrase of some current political popularity, we should "stay the course" as best as possible in this time of lesser public support.

One point in favor of this response is that it may well be easier to persevere in the roles of initiators and evaluators of juvenile justice policy than in the same roles for adult criminal justice. Corrado (1981: 27) makes the point that "unlike adult criminal justice policies, few politicians appear to be willing to give up on humanistic policy toward juveniles." If the kinds of new programs for juvenile justice that have been proposed recently are indicative, there is some evidence to support Corrado's claim. Indeed, the kinds of programs advocated now for juvenile justice seem to be a compromise between the gereral belief that treatment programs have failed to reduce crime and the unwillingness of politicians and the public to believe that children as a class are untreatable. That is, the effort to find "serious" or "career delinquents" seems to embody a belief that treatment programs have failed because they were not separately targeted to the incorrigible minority on the one hand and the treatable majority on the other. Moreover, as Platt (1964) argued, the idea of treatment historically has been part of the "child saver" philosophy of juvenile justice that has its roots in conservative ideology. Thus, even in times of conservative political dominance it is unlikely that juvenile justice will be asked to abandon a treatment orientation.

Although the ideas of initiating or evaluating new policy that is restricted in content by ideology or public attitudes may not appeal to many researchers, the alternatives of having programs initiated by persons who may have a limited working knowledge of juvenile justice or evaluated only by the ideologically commited may be less appealing. Furthermore, taking on these tasks may permit one to serve an educative function for politicians and the public. The point that some programs for social reform or treatment have not worked as intended does not mean that *any* program for punishment or deterrence will work has been made effectively in the academic "nothing works" dialogue (Gendrau and Ross, 1981). However, it seems likely that politicians and the public will pay more attention to the results of actual experiments in implementing "get tough" programs than they do to academic discourse. The educative potential of this kind of research is underscored in McDermott's discussion in this volume of research to identify and treat serious juvenile offenders. Much attention in recent years has been given to chronically violent youth, with the attendant belief that they are disproportionately responsible for juvenile crime. As McDermott notes, however, contrary to the myth of the prevalence of chronically violent youth, a large-scale project to identify serious juvenile offenders to be the subjects of experimentation with special treatment programs encountered major difficulty because not enough of them could be enlisted to support experimental research.

The injunction to stay the course also applies to disciplinary commitment to the enterprise of evaluation research itself and to the development of evaluation research methodology. Bearers of bad tidings frequently suffer from their hearers' desire to "shoot the messenger" and there is some indication of this sentiment concerning evaluation research in criminal justice (e.g., Hackler, 1978, 1979). There is a danger that a retreat from the field produced by a reduction in research funds may become full scale. Corrado (1981) offers several persuasive reasons for why it should not be, and perhaps the most telling is that lost in the nothing works discussion is the fact that evaluation studies have demonstrated that *some* programs do work. A lull in research activity provides the opportunity to scrutinize why research shows that some programs have worked and others have not. Positive or negative findings may result from the theory motivating a particular program, the operationalization of the program in practice, or in the research methods employed. Retreat from the fields provides an opportunity to consider the respective roles of the above factors in producing the collective body of results on specific criminal justice practices. In this regard the current attention to self-review and self criticism in the field may be benefical in the long run if its results in a codification of what we have and have not learned, and in an agenda for further research to address what we do not know.

Understanding the Sources of
the Public Mandate for Change

The second area of response to public mandates for change, I suggest, should be to seek a better understanding of the sources of public demands for change in criminal justice, with the aim of informing the public of what has been accomplished and encouraging public awareness of the problems and prospects of policy experimentation and evaluation. While substantial research attention has been paid to public fear of crime, research on other topics that may contribute to our understanding of the sources of public demand for specific policy—such as perceptions of criminal justice practice and beliefs about the causes of crime—is largely lacking (for a review of public opinion data in these areas, see Margarita and Parisi, 1979).

There are reasons for not being optimistic about the possibilities of changing public opinion to favor greater support for policy research. Perhaps the major reason lies in the seeming susceptibility of public beliefs about crime and criminal justice practice to political influence. One reading of trend data on public beliefs about crime and criminal justice supports an inference of their susceptibility to change in conformity with the ideological orientation of the party in power. The substantial decline in public endorsement of social reform and rehabilitation as the preferred methods of crime reduction and the increase in sentiment for get tough solutions, punishment and incarceration, in the 1970s (Margarita and Parisi, 1979; Flanagan et al., 1982) does, of course, coincide with a period of ascendency in the influence of conservative politics.

The association of public demands for tougher policy with the growth in the fortunes of conservative politics may well argue for efforts at political influence rather than direct appeals to the public. However, it is not clear from public opinion data alone that the growth in public sentiment for get tough solutions did not originate entirely or partly independent of political efforts to encourage it. An equally plausible interpretation of trend data is that the success of conservative politics was facilitated by independently growing public sentiment that liberal programs emphasizing social reform and treatment have failed to produce results. If public mandates for change have arisen independently of political efforts to shape them, then efforts at political influence, even if successful, may not be sufficient to renew political commitment to support for the broad-ranging policy research program established in the last two decades. Politicians are reluctant to support policy that visibly runs against public sentiment (Burnstein, 1979).

I suggest as a starting point in efforts to inform public opinion that much can be gained from attention to findings from the field of social cognition—specifically to research on what might be called ordinary or common principles of inference about cause (for an excellent review, see Nisbett and Ross, 1980).

Research in this area underscores the prevalence of certain errors of causal inference in common causal interpretation. To illustrate the potential benefit of this work for understanding the sources of public mandates for change, I discuss here the implications of four such errors for inferences about crime causation and public demands for change:

(1) *The fundamental attribution error*—the tendency to overemphasize disposi-tional causes (i.e., properties of individual actors such as personality traits and motivation) and underemphasize situational causes (supraindividual or struc-tural factors). In deriving the conclusion that greater deterrence and secure confinement are needed, the public seems to be assuming that the increase in the crime rate is due to an increase in the motivation of persons to commit crimes. The idea that crime has increased because the opportunities to commit crime have increased due to aggregate change is a lifestyle (fewer married persons, more women working), the ease of committing property crime, and so on (i.e., the opportunity theory of Cohen et al., 1980), for example, seems not to be part of public thinking about factors leading to increased crime.

(2) *The saliency principle*—in thinking about causation overemphasis is given to factors that are highly visible, immediate, or affect-laden relative to less salient causes. This principle seems to lie in part behind the public concern with finding and incarcerating violent criminals as a solution to the general crime problem, since violence has strong salience to persons.

(3) *The resemblance criterion*—is the assumption that causes should share the salient properties of or resemble the consequences. Since the consequences of crime are characterized as bad, it seems to be assumed that the causes of crime must also be inherently bad. This assumption leads to an ignorance of the possibilities that certain crimes may be committed as calculated rational acts, and that increases in crime may be the result of factors considered affectively neutral or positive—such as the increase in the proportion of working women, increasing affluence, the freedom permitted in a mobile society, and the like. It also seems to bias persons toward explanations of crime that involve postulated "bad" characteristics of persons or societies as its causes.

(4) *The principle of "hydraulic causation"*—persons may acknowledge the exis-tence of multiple causes, but they often act consistent with a unitary cause assumption by treating hypothesized causes as if they were in competition in a zero sum game. This principle may underlie the public rush to embrace deter-rence and incarceration as solutions to the crime problem. It appears that the public views the three major proposed solutions to the crime problem—social reform, treatment, and deterrence—as candidates competing for sufficiency as the cause of reduction in crime. Thus, assumed evidence that the first two solutions have failed is taken to mean that deterrence must work.

One general point from the above examples is that the logic of public reasoning about crime causation and control may be quite different from that employed by policy researchers. We cannot simply assume that the arguments we make to each other in support of the worth of a long-run commitment to policy research in criminal justice will be effective in convincing the public of the worth of this enterprise. To construct effective arguments to be placed before the public, we need to understand better the assumptions the public makes about crime and criminal justice and the principles of inference they use in deriving conclusions about what should be done to reduce crime.

OVERVIEW

The chapters in this volume focus on two areas of mandated change in juvenile justice policy in recent years. Chapters 2, 3, and 4 examine programs for either diverting certain youths from juvenile court (Chapters 2 and 3) or preventing and treating delinquency by means of community involvement (Chapter 4). Chapters 5, 6, 7, and 8 focus on the more contemporary concern with identifying and treating or controlling the serious juvenile offender.

The chapters by Rausch and Logan and by Saul and Davidson present findings from ongoing juvenile diversion projects concerning the potential unintended negative consequences of these programs in practice of widening the scope of involvement with juvenile justice rather than the intended reduction. Both studies find evidence for some widening of scope, and propose that this unintended negative consequence stems from the operating philosophy and organizational imperatives of current juvenile justice systems. The authors differ somewhat in their conclusions. Saul and Davidson conclude that diversion programs as currently implemented are of ambiguous value, but they may benefit their clients if the means to avoid current problems of implementation were overcome. Rausch and Logan, on the other hand, conclude that the results of diversion programs in practice largely argue for favoring decriminalizing status offenses over efforts to divert status offenders.

Morash discusses the issues involved in and presents research findings on the use of existing community programs to prevent and control delinquent behavior. This research examines adolescent self-reports of involvement and experience with community programs in two parts of Boston. Morash concludes with a discussion of common errors in thinking about the potential effectiveness of community programs for juvenile corrections, and the implications of these errors for producing results that are less effective in the real world than thought to be in the ideal world.

The chapter by McDermott provides a critical discussion of one aspect of the contemporary mandated attention to treating or controlling the serious juvenile offender—defining criteria for categorizing and selecting juveniles for special handling as serious offenders. McDermott's extensive discussion of the practical, conceptual, legal, and moral issues involved in defining and selecting serious juvenile offenders cautions against any rush to embrace programs targeted at this group as a simple solution to juvenile crime problem. Such programs are potentially beneficial to serious and nonserious offenders, to juvenile practitioners, and to the public, but McDermott cautions that there are many issues and questions that policy researchers and practitioners must address as they consider implementing them.

The next two chapters present findings from studies of juveniles who make up part of the group conventionally labeled "serious juvenile offenders." Fagan et al. (Chapter 6) use data collected as part of the Violent Juvenile Offender Program to profile characteristics of chronically violent juvenile youths. Further, they present the rudiments of an integrated theory of violent delinquency. Feldman and Caplinger (Chapter 7) present results of an experiment to evaluate the effectiveness of treating antisocial youths in integrated groups, composed predominantly of prosocial youths. The motivation for their research came from the observation that the typical program for antisocial youths, whether conducted in institutions or in a community setting, involves treatment among peers also identified as antisocial and thus provides plentiful deviant role models and peer reinforcements for antisocial behavior.

The last chapter concerns gang violence, a problem that for several reasons seems to have special salience for the public and the mass media. Maxson and Klein describe the structure of a gang intervention program developed in accord with the current emphasis in criminal justice on deterrence. Their description of the numerous problems that have developed in the short history of this intervention again underscores the point that the lack of success of treatment or social reform programs does not guarantee that any deterrence program will be effective. Problems of implementing such programs due to interinstitutional conflict, the political nature of interventions, media involvement, and so on characterized past gang intervention programs and continue to place limits on the success of contemporary, deterrence-oriented gang intervention efforts.

REFERENCES

BURNSTEIN, P. (1979) "Public opinion, demonstrations, and the passage of antidiscrimination legislation." Public Opinion Quarterly 79: 157-172.

CAMPBELL, D. T. (1969) "Reforms as experiments." American Psychologist 24: 409-429.

COHEN, L. E., M. FELSON, and K. LAND (1980) "Property crime rates in the United States: a macrodynamic analysis, 1947-1977; with ex ante forecasts for the mid-1980s." American Journal of Sociology 86: 90-118.

CORRADO, R. R. (1981) "Using experiments in evaluating delinquency prevention programs," in R. Roesch and R. R. Corrado (eds.) Evaluation and Criminal Justice Policy. Beverly Hills, CA: Sage.

FISHMAN, R. (1977) "An evaluation of criminal recidivism in projects providing rehabilitation and diversion services in New York City." Journal of Criminal Law and Criminology 68: 283-305.

FLANAGAN, T. J., D. J. van ALSTYNE, and M. R. GOTTFREDSON (1982) Sourcebook of Criminal Justice Statistics—1981. U.S. Department of Justice, Bureau of Justice Statistics. Washington, DC: Government Printing Office.

GENDRAU, P. and R. R. ROSS (1981) "Correctional potency: treatment and deterrence on trial," in R. Roesch and R. R. Corrado (eds.) Evaluation and Criminal Justice Policy. Beverly Hills, CA: Sage.

GOTTFREDSON, M. R. (1982) "The social scientist and rehabilitative crime policy." Criminology 20: 29-42.

——— (1979) "Treatment destruction techniques." Journal of Research in Crime Delinquency 16: 39-54.

HACKLER, J. (1979) "Invitation to error: the dangers of evaluation and some alternatives." Canadian Journal of Criminology 21: 39-51.

——— (1978) The Prevention of Crime: The Great Stumble Forward. Toronto: Methuen.

JENSEN, G. F. (1981) Sociology and Delinquency: Current Issues. Beverly Hills, CA: Sage.

MARGARITA, M. and N. PARISI (1979) Public Opinion and Criminal Justice: Selected Issues and Trends. Working Paper. Albany, NY: Criminal Justice Research Center.

MARTINSON, R. (1974) "What works?—Questions and answers about prison reform." The Public Interest 35: 22-54.

NISBETT, R. and L. ROSS (1980) Human Inference: Strategies and Shortcomings of Social Judgement. Englewood Cliffs, NJ: Prentice-Hall.

PALMER, T. (1975) "Martinson revisited." Journal of Research in Crime and Delinquency 12: 133-152.

PLATT, A. (1969) The Child Savers: The Invention of Delinquency. Chicago: University of Chicago Press.

ROESCH, R. and R. R. CORRADO (1981) "Evaluation and criminal justice policy," in R. Roesch and R. R. Corrado (eds.) Evaluation and Criminal Justice Policy. Beverly Hills, CA: Sage.

——— (1979) "The policy implications of evaluation research: some issues raised by the Fishman study of rehabilitation and diversion services." Journal of Criminal Law and Criminology 70: 530-541.

ROSSI, P. H., R. A. BERK, and K. J. LENIHAN (1980) Money, Work and Crime: Some Experimental Results. New York: Academic Press.

WILSON, J. Q. (1975) Thinking About Crime. New York: Basic Books.

2

Sharla P. Rausch
Social Policy Research

Charles H. Logan
University of Connecticut

DIVERSION FROM JUVENILE COURT
Panacea or Pandora's Box?

The same humanitarian concern that gave rise to the juvenile court requires a continuing critical appraisal of whether it is indeed achieving humanitarian goals. Widespread disenchantment with the juvenile justice system reflects the belief that juvenile courts are ineffective and stigmatizing. Proponents of the labeling perspective suggest that possible stigmatizing effects of juvenile court processing may promote rather than prevent further delinquent activity (Lemert, 1971). Others point out that youths not charged with a criminal act may be confined with youths detained on more serious charges, exposure that may result in the acquisition of delinquent skills among the newly initiated (Thomas, 1976). These considerations have prompted the President's Crime Commission (1967: 27) to question the jurisdiction of the juvenile court over "status offenses" (i.e., conduct illegal only for children) and to recommend a search for alternatives.

Diversion and decriminalization are two alternatives to juvenile court processing that have been suggested with regard to status offenders and their acts. Decriminalization calls for repeal of the legal rules defining status offenses as delinquent (Empey, 1976: 38), while diversion entails removal of status

AUTHORS' NOTE: This research was supported by grants from the National Institue for Juvenile Justice and Delinquency Prevention of the Law Enforcement Assistance Administration, 76JN-99-0015 and 76JN-99-1003. This financial support does not necessarily indicate the concurrence of NIJJDP in any of the statements or conclusions presented here. We are indebted to Albert K. Cohen for a critical reading of an earlier draft.

offenders from juvenile court processing—usually to some structured form of treatment (Bullington et al., 1978: 59). Rather than the more radical strategy of decriminalization, diversion has been adopted as the usual response to the status offender dilemma. In particular, there has been a proliferation of diversion programs in response to the Juvenile Justice and Delinquency Prevention Act of 1974 and the resulting LEAA funding.

In this chapter we will argue that decriminalization is a more logical response to the problem of status offenses than is diversion. The objections to diversion are both practical and philosophical; we will illustrate both types, using as our example a status offender diversion (or "deinstitutionalization") project in Connecticut. To demur in advance, we will not claim that our data and methods are strong enough to establish firmly the existence of the practical problems warned of in prior research on diversion, but they will be consistent with and supportive of those warnings. Likewise, we do not wish to raise the expectation at the outset that we will be able to resolve fully the philosophical, political, and policy dilemmas entailed in efforts at juvenile diversion, but we do intend to address them explicitly in a way that most discussions of diversion do not. By using the Connecticut project as a concrete example, we plan to show that diversion programs, as distinct from decriminalization efforts, are likely to aggravate the very kinds of intrusive intervention they are ostensibly designed to avoid.

ISSUES IN DIVERSION

Proponents of diversion contend both that it is morally wrong to prosecute juveniles for noncriminal behavior (Thomas, 1976; American Friends Service Committee, 1971) and that the stigmatizing effects of court processing may result in commitment to a delinquent role (Lemert, 1971). However, if it is morally wrong to process status offenders judicially, then it would seem to follow that they should not be subject to the judicial system in the first place, which would obviate any need for diversion. Hence, this principle cannot be used logically as a rationale for diversion; it is more appropriate as a rationale for decriminalization. Current enthusiasm for diversion rests more distinctively on a belief in the negative labeling effects of juvenile court processing, particularly with regard to noncriminal offenders. Diversion programs hold out the promise of individualized treatment without stigmatization—the same unfulfilled promise the juvenile court has offered since its inception (Platt, 1977).

The hypothesized negative labeling effect of juvenile court processing, although theoretically appealing, has received little sound empirical support. Mahoney (1974) concludes that the results of such studies are, at best, conflicting. Studies supportive of the labeling perspective have been fraught with methodological weaknesses that have diminished the validity of their findings. (The same is true of research critical of the labeling perspective, but it is support that is at issue here.) Only the weakest support for the labeling perspective could be found in Tittle's (1975a) critique of the more methodologically sound studies or in Thomas's (1977) recent research on the effects of labeling on subsequent delinquent behavior. In fact, some studies suggest that labeling may have positive (i.e., crime-reducing) effects (Mahoney, 1974; Thorsell and Klemke, 1972; Tittle, 1975). In short, the research to date has been inconsistent and inconclusive in its findings. Moreover, it is consistent with the principles of labeling theory (Schur, 1971) to believe that diversion to a special program may have the same stigmatizing effect as the juvenile court. The label may merely change (e.g., from "delinquent" to "child in need of supervision") without any change in consequences. It should be recalled that the label "delinquent" was itself adopted in an attempt to avoid the stigma of the label "criminal" (Platt, 1977; Stapleton and Teitelbaum, 1972).

One common component of all rationales for diversion seems to be that *less* intervention is better than *more* intervention. Thus, whatever else it involves, diversion necessarily implies an attempt to make the form of social control more limited in scope. Studies of diversion programs, however, indicate that instead of limiting the scope of the system, diversion programs often broaden it. They do this either by intensifying services or by taking in more cases. The latter is referred to as a "widening of the net" effect. Police and court intake personnel are often reluctant to subject youths to the juvenile justice system; at the same time, they may be reluctant simply to ignore them or turn them loose. When provided with a formal channel for diversion, police and court intake officers have been directing to this channel many individuals who otherwise would have been left alone or released at the intake stage (Lundman, 1976; Gibbons and Blake, 1976; Klein and Teilman, 1976).

In interviews with police, Klein et al. (1976: 107) found that police criteria for diversion consisted of low seriousness of offense, a willingness to be referred, shorter prior arrest records (two priors or less), younger offenders, and a preference for youths seen as unlikely to be rearrested. In essence, the diverted population was drawn from a pool of offenders who, prior to the implementation of diversion programs, would probably have been released or left alone. The effect of such a policy has been to expand control over a larger, less seriously involved sector of the juvenile population.

Diversion programs may also have an intensified or excessive treatment effect. One study looking at three cohorts of offenders diverted to noncourt agencies contrasted to a comparable group for whom court petitions were filed found that diverted offenders received "means of seven, eight and a half, and almost twelve hours of counseling," while almost all of those youths for whom court petitions were filed were either released or put on informal probation

(Klein et al., 1976: 110). Blomberg (1977: 278) also found that diversion personnel rarely closed a case at the first meeting. He suggested that "this tendency might well reflect the fear at the program's inception that not providing services would undermine the need for the diversion program." He also found that when clients or their families failed to cooperate fully with the intervention services, diversion personnel had a strong tendency to respond by petitioning the court to remove the child from the home.

From the studies so far, it would appear that diversion programs have a potential for increasing rather than reducing the state's control over juveniles. Instead of diverting youngsters from state-imposed or state-sponsored treatment systems, these programs may be drawing more of them into these systems as a means of providing services. Seen in this light, diversion may not be the panacea it sometimes claims to be. There is no solid evidence to support the contention that diversion will reduce the potential for stigmatization; it can be incompatible with due process of law; and it may result in greater social control rather than less. Instead of a panacea, diversion may be a Pandora's box.

DATA AND MEASURES

The purpose of this study was to understand better the system impact of diversion as practiced during the Connecticut Deinstitutionalization of Status Offenders (DSO) project. Connecticut was one of several sites whose programs for deinstitutionalization of status offenders were approved by LEAA. It was the goal of the Connecticut program to divert status offenders from detention or correctional facilities into alternative forms of treatment. Three treatment models (one in each of the state's court districts) were implemented: (1) a community-based minimum intervention model in which community contractors provided a maximum of five family crisis intervention counseling sessions to DSO clients; (2) a court-based community minimum intervention model in which court personnel likewise provided a maximum of five family crisis intervention counseling sessions to DSO clients; and (3) a maximum intervention model in which an individualized treatment program was developed for each DSO client. Although these models were labeled "minimum" and "maximum" intervention, those were relative terms, since even the maximum intervention model was intended as an alternative to the supposedly more intrusive juvenile court system. Thus, these three DSO treatment models should be compared not only with each other but with a preprogram group of status offenders who received normal court processing but who met the eligibility criteria that were to be in effect during the DSO program period. Under these criteria, all status offenders coming to detention were considered eligible except the following: (a) juveniles whose instant offense included charges other than a status offense; (b) juveniles with prior criminal charges still pending; and (c) status offenders who were already under the supervision of the Juvenile Court at the time of detention.

The DSO program has been evaluated elsewhere (Logan, et al., 1978) to assess the effects of the treatment models, as well as some of the effects of the program on the juvenile justice system as a whole. Using data collected for that evaluation, the focus of this study was on the effects of diversion on client flow and degree of intervention. Specifically, we were interested in whether or not the availability of services led to an increase in the number (or change in the type) of children brought into the system, or to an increase in control exerted over these children through expanded services and removal from the home.

Both quantitative and qualitative methods were employed to obtain the necessary data. Data collected from computerized juvenile court records served as the quantitative data source. Interviews at various levels of program implementation provided the qualitative material.

Client flow was defined for both preprogram and program time periods as the number and composition of status offenders entering the court system. This was operationalized as the number referred, number and proportion of referrals who were detained, and proportion of detainees having no prior referrals.

Intervention was defined as the degree to which program services were provided, length of time status offenders were "under supervision or control," and the extent to which removal from home occurred. The only groups for which we had comparable measures on all three of these dimensions of intervention were the two minimum intervention models. Thus, our analysis of the effects of diversion on intervention was not a comparison of diversion with regular court processing. Rather, it was a comparison of two different types of diversion: one administered by a juvenile court and one administered by private agencies. This has the advantage of comparing court versus private agency administration where goals are officially the same. For these two minimum intervention models, the degree of service provision was operationalized as the number of family crisis intervention counseling sessions. Length of time under supervision was measured by the number of days from the first crisis intervention counseling session to the last. Removal from home was measured by the proportion of cases using temporary shelter and the median number of days spent in temporary shelter.

RESULTS

Client Flow and Composition

To determine if there was a "widening of the net" effect, we compared program and preprogram status offenders with regard to the number referred, number detained, and proportion of status offense referrals detained. There was little difference between the preprogram and program periods with regard to the number of status offenders referred to juvenile court (1847 and 1837 referrals, respectively). However, there was a small increase in the number and proportion of status offenders *detained* following the implementation of the DSO program. Of those status offenders referred to juvenile court during the preprogram period 430 (or 23%) were detained, while 522 (or 28%) of those status offenders referred during the program period were detained.

Although this difference in proportion detained is statistically significant at the .02 level and is in the predicted direction, it is too small (5 points) to support more than a weak form of the net-widening hypothesis. Perhaps the safest conclusion is that there is no strong evidence that the implementation of the DSO program resulted in more than a negligible increase in the referral and detention of status offenders.

From interviews, we identified two possible factors that may have helped to prevent a widening of the net effect. First, due to predictions that there would be increased delivery of status offenders to detention in order to receive the special services of the diversion program, the project director strongly requested that police officers not do this. Second, a detention center intake officer suggested to us that there may have been an implicit quota on status offenders, based on offense seriousness and bed space considerations. At any rate, there was little change in the number of status offenders referred or the proportion detained following program implementation.

Another aspect of client flow suggested by the diversion literature is the displacement of some youths who would ordinarily have been inserted into the juvenile justice system by the referral for treatment of juveniles who would otherwise have been left alone or released at the initial stage of processing. As one test of this possibility, we compared the proportion of status offender "novices"—those having no prior referrals—for the preprogram and DSO program periods of time.

The two time periods were found to be comparable with regard to the proportion of novices among status offense *referrals* (44% versus 48%). The advent of the DSO program, however, coincided with a considerable shift in the proportion of *detainees* who were novices, from 29% to 44%. This increase in detention of status offenders having no prior record suggests that many of those status offenders who previously would have been released or referred without detention were being detained during the DSO period. Note, however, that the total number of referrals remained virtually the same and that the total percentage detained increased by only five points, while the percentage of novices among the referrals only increased by four points. Since the number and composition of referrals remained virtually unchanged, the 15-point increase in the percentage of novices among detainees suggests that during the time of the DSO program, if police began bringing to detention novices whom they would previously have released, they must also have begun releasing at least some veterans whom they would previously have detained. In other words, the police were replacing veterans with novices in the detention case flow. This would not fit in with the total pattern unless the police were not simply releasing the veterans but relabeling them and inserting them into the court system as other delinquents rather than as status offenders.

In any case, it appears that during the DSO program period police brought to detention status offenders whom they would not previously have—perhaps in order to gain for them the treatment provided by the DSO program. Thus, while the Connecticut DSO program does not appear to have had much effect on the number of status offenders referred to court and only a tiny effect on the proportion detained, it does appear to have affected the type of status offender selected for detention with an eye toward diversion.[1]

Intervention

Critics of diversion contend that instead of limiting control over status offenders, diversion programs may extend it through expanded services and removal from the home. Unfortunately, problems in availability and comparability of data made it impossible for us to compare the preprogram court processing with the DSO diversion programs on similar measures of intervention, control, and servicing. Moreover, one of the DSO treatment models (the maximum intervention model), though intended as a form of diversion from court, was definitely not designed to reduce the total degree of intervention. However, the two minimum intervention models of the DSO program were designed to be comparable in every respect except one: administration by community agencies versus administration by the juvenile court. Thus, apart from the question of whether either of these diversion models was less intrusive than regular court processing, we can at least examine the effect of juvenile court sponsorship and involvement in a diversion program that is attempting, by design, to be minimally intrusive. This is actually an important comparison, because one of the unexamined assumptions of diversion programs is that the juvenile court (and perhaps any state agency) is intrusive by its very nature rather than by virtue of its goals. Thus, our comparison here allows us to test this assumption in a context where the goal of minimum intervention is held constant but the legal character of the administrative agent varies.

We compared the court-based and community-based minimum intervention models with respect to the number of family crisis intervention counseling sessions per case, time from first counseling session to last, median stay in program, proportion of program cases using temporary shelter, and median stay in temporary shelter. Given the small number of cases in the community-based model, the comparative results can only be viewed as suggestive; but even by itself the pattern for the court-based model (with the larger N) is instructive.

Although both the community-based and court-based models were intended to offer a minimal number of family crisis intervention counseling sessions, with a maximum of five, Table 2.1 indicates that there was a difference between the court and community contractors in the distribution of the number of counseling sessions. The community contractors leaned away from a smaller number of sessions. Only 6% of their cases received the absolute minimum of one, and only 18% received no more than two. About a quarter of their cases received the maximum number of five sessions. In contrast, the court counselors tended toward either the minimum or the maximum number of sessions. One-fifth of the court cases received the absolute minimum and another fifth received only two sessions. While 30% of the court cases were given the maximum of five sessions, this is not greatly different from the community cases (24%).

Community counselors voiced particular dissatisfaction with the minimum intervention model. They admitted unofficially that they did not believe in it and were uncomfortable basing their reputations on such a minumum treatment of the child. Contractors in both models also indicated that many of the children coming to them had serious emotional problems and were in need of services to a greater extent than could be offered by the diversion models.

Although on the whole the community-based contractors tended to stretch their cases out over a longer period, Table 2.1 indicates that in both models over half of the cases were held open a month or more and a significant portion were held open for over two months. The median stay in the community-based program was 27 days, and 32 days in the court-based program.

With regard to removal from home, both the court and community minimum intervention models made considerable use of temporary shelter. Table 2.1 shows that temporary shelter use ranged from 11% of the cases, with a median of 2.5 days in the community-based model, to 27% of the cases, with a median of 13.2 days in the court-based model. These findings are all the more interesting when we note that under normal court processing during the preprogram period, status offenders were released from detention within a median of 2 days (Logan et al., 1978: 120).

In some ways the court-based diversion was less intrusive (more cases with minimal counseling, more cases with a short time in the program) and in other ways more intrusive (slightly more cases with maximal counseling, more cases in temporary shelter and for longer periods) than the community-based diversion. There seems to be no necessary connection between juvenile court and greater intervention *when goals are held constant.* At the same time, it is clear that diversion itself can be intrusive, regardless of the agency in charge. The

TABLE 2.1   Court versus Noncourt Minimum Intervention

	Community Minimum	Court Minimum
Counseling Sessions		
1	6% (1)	20% (18)
2	12% (2)	20% (18)
3	29% (5)	18% (16)
4	29% (5)	12% (10)
5	24% (4)	30% (27)
Average	(3.5)	(3.1)
First to Last Session (days)		
0-7	6% (1)	16% (15)
8-14	6% (1)	11% (10)
15-21	17% (3)	9% (9)
22-28	17% (3)	14% (13)
29-60	44% (8)	36% (34)
61+	10% (2)	14% (13)
Highest	(138)	(206)
Median	(32)	(27)
Temporary shelter	11% (2)	27% (25)
Median Stay (days)	(2.5)	(13.2)

minimum intervention models were often implemented as maximally as the model designs allowed, with a desire on the part of the contractors for even greater service provision. In addition to the tendency of the minimum intervention contractors to use the maximum number of sessions allowed, there was a proclivity toward holding cases open for long periods. DSO clients were also removed from home for longer periods than preprogram cases, especially in the court-based model. Thus, it would appear that instead of limiting intervention into the lives of status offenders, the Connecticut diversion program increased it.

CONCLUSION

This study suggests that diversion may not be the panacea its proponents claim it to be. Although we found no clear proof that the implementation of a diversion program resulted in an overall widening of the net, there was some indication that during the program novice status offenders may have been substituted for some veteran status offenders at detention centers—possibly to gain the services offered by the DSO project.

There was also evidence that diversion can be as intrusive as normal court processing. DSO cases spent time comparable to preprogram cases under control or supervision, and there was a greater tendency to remove program youths from home. For the most part, there was also a tendency on the part of the minimum intervention contractors to provide their intervention in the most maximal way allowed by the model design.

Apparently, whether rightly or wrongly, child helpers are reluctant to let go or leave be. Rather than necessarily limiting the scope of social control, diversion can maintain or broaden it. If diversion merely replaces the juvenile court with other agencies of intervention, it may be necessary to fight again on new ground the battles that have only recently led to the clarification and enforcement of rights that were found necessary to protect the youth from his helpers in the juvenile court.

The only way to ensure against all possible tendencies toward beneficent despotism in diversion programs is to make participation in them truly voluntary on the part of clients. This was hardly the case in the Connecticut program. Although court charges were dropped for all clients entering the DSO program, thus removing them from the justice system, the only alternative was continued detention and/or further court processing. During the design stage of the DSO project and at a later point, one of the authors suggested to the appropriate authorities that all juveniles eligible for the diversion program should first have all charges dropped and *only then* be invited to partake of the DSO-sponsored services. This suggestion was not taken seriously on either occasion; in fact, it was met with derision. The youths' options were also limited by the necessity for parental consent to DSO treatment. Parents often wanted their children to remain in the custody of the court "to teach them a lesson." Some of the parents who agreed to the program felt themselves, as well as their children, to be subject to the court's authority, and a few program personnel openly admitted that they found useful the parents' and clients' mistaken impression that failure to cooperate with program services could result in automatic re-referral to court. The confusion between court and diversion program was presumably strongest under the court-based minimum intervention model. Although technically the probation officers who counseled DSO clients did so as subcontractors to the Department of Children and Youth Services, there can be little doubt that they saw themselves, as did the clients and their parents, primarily as probation officers.

It is hard to escape the conclusion that no matter how they are designed, diversion programs are likely to be seen as extensions, or alternate forms, of the juvenile court. Indeed, this perception is basically accurate. The only genuine alternative to juvenile court is decriminalization, not diversion. In the absence of decriminalization, the closest a diversion program can come to fulfilling its intended purpose is first to drop all charges and exclude all possibility of future court processing for the behavior or situation that led to intervention initially and then (and only then) offer all services on a completely voluntary basis.

NOTE

1. We did not have data that would allow us to determine stability of the percentage of novices among detainees from year to year in the absence of any special program. From 29% to 44%, however, is a 50% increase and it does not seem likely that all of it could be the result of random fluctuation. A more serious problem—one found in any "before-and-after" design—is the difficulty in ruling out the possibility that an independently changing climate could account for some discovered shift even if the program in question had not existed. While we know of no changes in law, political climate, agency policy, public opinion, or other variables that could account for the shift we discovered, this is negative rather than positive "evidence." However, insofar as there was any discernible preexisting trend in policy and opinion, it was in a direction different from our findings. Connecticut, as elsewhere in the United States, was becoming sensitive to the issue of deinstitutionalization and could see the federal handwriting on the wall: "States Shall Not Lock Up Status Offenders Or They Will Lose Federal Money." Thus, a changing climate hypothesis would lead us to expect a decrease in referrals and detentions of status offenders. Instead, we get a change in the nature of status offenders detained, which is difficult to explain other than as a reclassificational response to the program.

REFERENCES

American Friends Service Committee (1971) Struggle for Justice. New York: Hill and Wang.
BLOMBERG, T. (1977) "Diversion and accelerated social control." Journal of Criminal Law and Criminology 68: 274-282.
BULLINGTON, B., J. SPROWLS, D. KATKIN, and M. PHILLIPS (1978) "A critique of diversionary juvenile justice." Crime and Delinquency 24: 59-71.
EMPEY, L. (1976) "The social construction of childhood, delinquency and social reform," pp. 27-54 in M. Klein (ed.) The Juvenile Justice System. Beverly Hills, CA: Sage.
GIBBONS, D. and G. BLAKE (1976) "Evaluating the impact of juvenile diversion programs." Crime and Delinquency 22: 411-420.
KLEIN, M., K. TEILMANN, J. STYLES, S. LINCOLN, and S. LABINROSENWIG (1976) "The explosion in police diversion programs: evaluating the structural dimensions of a social fad," pp. 101-119 in M. Klein (ed.) The Juvenile Justice System. Beverly Hills, CA: Sage.
KLEIN, M. and K. TEILMAN (1976) Pivotal Ingredients of Police Juvenile Diversion Programs. National Institute for Juvenile Justice and Delinquency Prevention.
LEMERT, E. (1971) Instead of Court: Diversion in Juvenile Justice. Rockville, MD: National Institute of Mental Health.
LOGAN, C., J. BACEWICZ, and S. RAUSCH (1978) An Evaluation of Connecticut's Deinstitutionalization of Status Offenders Program. University of Connecticut.
LUNDMAN, R. (1976) "Will diversion reduce recidivism?" Crime and Delinquency 22: 421-427.
MAHONEY, A. (1974) "The effect of labeling upon youths in the juvenile justice system." Law and Society Review 8: 583-614.
PLATT, A. (1977) The Child Savers. Chicago: University of Chicago Press.

President's Commission on Law Enforcement and Administration of Justice (1967) Task Force Report: Juvenile Delinquency and Youth Crime. Washington, DC: Government Printing Office.

SCHUR, E. (1971) Labeling Deviant Behavior: Its Sociological Implications. NY: Harper & Row.

STAPLETON, W. and L. TEITELBAUM (1972) In Defense of Youth. NY: Russell Sage Foundation.

THOMAS, C. (1977) The Effect of Legal Sanctions on Juvenile Delinquency. A Comparison of the Labeling and Deterrence Perspectives. Bowling Green, OH: Bowling Green State University.

——— (1976) "Are status offenders really so different?" Crime and Delinquency 22: 438-455.

THORSELL, B. and L. KLEMKE (1972) "The labeling process: reinforcement or deterrent? Law and Society Review 6: 393-402.

TITTLE, C. (1975a) "Labeling and crime: an empirical evaluation," pp. 157-179 in W. Gove (ed.) The Labeling of Deviance: Evaluating A Perspective. New York: John Wiley.

——— (1975) "Deterrents or labeling?" Social Forces 53: 399-410.

John A. Saul

William S. Davidson II

Michigan State University

3

IMPLEMENTATION OF JUVENILE DIVERSION PROGRAMS
Cast Your Net on the Other Side of the Boat

Researchers concerned with social problems have recently become more aware that unintended negative consequences can result from social reform programs (Caplan and Nelson, 1973; Gaylin et al., 1978; Klein, 1979; Rappaport, 1981). Whether through faulty design or faulty implementation, social programs may actually serve to exacerbate the problems they were supposed to solve. Concerns of this type have been increasingly expressed about the impact of diversion programs on the juvenile justice system. Diversion programs were originally intended as positive alternatives to the juvenile justice system, a social institution whose own reformist ideals were said to have turned sour (U.S. President's Commission, 1967; in re Gault, 1967; James, 1969; Gold and Williams, 1969). However, the extent to which diversion programs actually achieve their goals must be evaluated before they can be considered as effective or true alternatives to traditional handling of youth in legal jeopardy. Hence, the purpose of this research is to examine the major unintended consequence of juvenile diversion: the possibility that diversion programs, rather than diverting youth away from the justice system, actually "widen the net" of justice system control over more youth.

The potential net-widening effect of diversion programs has attracted considerable attention in the literature. The term refers to the process by which diversion programs result in an increase in the number of young people under

AUTHORS' NOTE: This work was completed under a grant from the Center for the Studies of Crime and Delinquency, National Institute of Mental Health (#MH29160).

the supervision or control of justice system agencies. Net-widening occurs when a youth who ordinarily would have been warned and released by the police or the juvenile court is instead referred to a diversion program. This, of course, represents the exact opposite of diversion's original intent, which was to provide alternative services to youths who typically would have come under further court supervision.

If the net-widening phenomenon is widespread, then diversion programs are not serving their intended type of client. This means that diversion in its true form has been neither actually implemented nor adequately tested (Klein, 1979). Evaluation of diversion program effects on individual-level outcomes such as recidivism becomes relatively meaningless because court-processed comparison cases would not be similar types of youths (Gibbons and Blake, 1976). In addition, diversion programs would lose their potential for cost savings because they would not be lessening the number of youths receiving police and court services (Rutherford and McDermott, 1976). Further, official delinquency rates could actually increase because greater numbers of youths would be monitored by justice system agencies. Youths referred to diversion have been said to be more susceptible to the negative consequences of justice system labeling, which may also lead to greater delinquency (Klein et al., 1979). Finally, diversion programming for those who would have been released outright may represent an abuse of individual rights due to the greater intrusiveness of the treatment (Howlett, 1973).

It is important to note here that in the practice of so-called true diversion one consequence would not occur. That is, if diversion were operationalized as diversion without services, then even unintended targets of diversion would not be drawn into the supervision of any formal agency of authority. However, the point is made moot by the extreme rarity of true diversion (Cressey and McDermott, 1974).Diversion *programs* (with services) thus have the potential for net-widening if they serve the wrong set of individuals.

Net-widening also makes evaluation of diversion program effects on recidivism difficult. Even if some of the intended set of individuals are diverted, their potential improvement will be disguised by the presence of unintended cases. Juveniles with few or no prior offenses cannot make much improvement on their record; it is therefore difficult to show results indicating reduced recidivism (Palmer and Lewis, 1980). The overall rate of delinquent behavior of diversion program cases may be lower due to the inclusion of low-risk youth, but there can be little chance of showing positive change over time.

Thus, the net-widening effects of diversion can have potentially serious consequences. Despite the importance of this issue, few empirical studies have evaluated diversion programs for evidence of net-widening. In contrast, many articles deal with the issue on a conceptual basis only, presenting no original data (Bullington et al., 1978; Nejelski, 1976; Klapmuts, 1974; Blomberg, 1980). Pabon (1978) characterized the available research on net-widening as being "impressionistic." Others have also noted the paucity and inadequacy of the research to date (Blomberg, 1977; Gibbons and Blake, 1976; Rutherford and McDermott, 1976). This problem can be attributed at least partly to an overemphasis on individual-level outcomes, occurring at the expense of system-level evaluation (Seidman, 1980; Wresinski et al., 1980). For a more complete examination of the relevant literature, see Saul (1981).

The present research attempts to fill the need for more conclusive empirical evidence on the net-widening phenomenon. By developing a more comprehensive evaluation strategy, the research also provides methods for improving the quality of future evaluations of diversion. Specifically, the study applies a comprehensive multimethod evaluation strategy to the assessment of possible net-widening effects of one ongoing juvenile diversion program.

The mulitimethod approach tests four variations of net-widening assessment methods. Each presents a different type of evidence for the basic question under investigation: Is this diversion program serving the intended set of juveniles— those who would otherwise have received further formal court processing? The four methods test the following hypotheses:

(1) If diversion is occurring as planned, diversion project control group cases returned to intake referees for an alternative disposition will receive further court processing.

(2) If diversion is occurring as planned, the characteristics of diversion cases should match up better with cases receiving further court processing than with those dismissed at intake.

(3) If diversion is occurring as planned, intake referees will tend to choose further court processing as their preferred alternative disposition for each diversion referral case.

(4) If diversion is occurring as planned, and all other factors remain constant, the proportion of cases handled formally by the court should decrease after the initiation of the diversion program.

METHOD

Setting

The diversion program under study is the Adolescent Diversion Project (ADP), which has been operating in a midwestern urban area since late 1976. The ADP was designed with the intention of avoiding net-widening, and thus provided an excellent setting for assessing the extent of net-widening in a well-intentioned and well-designed program. Youngsters were eligible for referral to the project only if they admitted guilt to a petitioned offense, were not guilty of severe injury-to-person crimes, were not already on formal court probation, and would not have been otherwise dismissed by the court at intake.

Because of the experimental design of the program, youths were randomly assigned to either the experimental or control group after referral by the intake referee at the court. Control group youths were returned to the referee for an alternative disposition, over which the ADP staff had no control. Experimental youth were assigned to volunteers, who were typically college students engaged in a field-experience course at the large state university in town or the local community college. The volunteers were trained in behavioral contracting and advocacy skills and supervised by ADP staff members throughout their 18-week intervention with the juveniles. The research presented here covers the first seven groups of youths referred by the court for diversion over a three-year period from late 1976 to early 1980. The project has contined to operate since that time, but relevant data are not yet available for the subsequent years.

Method 1—Analysis of Control Group Dispositions

There were 62 control group cases during the project's first seven groups of referrals. Court files were examined to check for their eventual dispositions.

Method 2—Discriminant Analysis of a Random Sample of Court Cases

Archival data from court files was collected to study court decision making. A random sample of about 14% of the intake disposition decisions occurring from late 1976 to late 1979 was collected to correspond with the period of the program under examination. This procedure resulted in the sampling of 364 cases. Cases that were on formal probation or institutional placement at the time of the sampled preliminary hearing were dropped from the sample as ineligible for referral to the diversion program. Also dropped were cases that previously had been referred to the program at some point. The sample was reduced to 253 cases after excluding these types of cases. All ADP cases were sampled for comparision purposes. These totalled 268 cases, although 20 had to be dropped due to missing court records. Various kinds of information were collected, including type and seriousness of offense, prior records, demographics, and parents' comments at the intake hearing. Reliability of coding was measured by the percentage of agreement on each variable. Variables ranged from 56% to 100% in reliability, with about half the variables at 90% or better.

On the basis of a discriminant analysis, it was determined which variables combined to best distinguish cases released at intake from those that received further court processing. The discriminating functions that best predicted group membership for the random decision sample were then applied to ADP cases. The discriminant analysis computer program then classified ADP cases into one of the groups based on the data collected on distinguishing variables. Diversion cases were then checked for the proportions that appeared similar to either the released-at-intake group, the adjourned-informal probation group, or the formal processing group. Actual informal probation was rarely used at this court, at least in the legal sense. Instead, juveniles were often placed under the intake worker's observation and supervision while their hearing was adjourned 30 days. For analytical purposes, these two types of court treatment were considered indentical. The distinction appears to be only procedural in nature, the youth in question experiencing the same degree of court supervision.

Method 3—Analysis of Questionnaire Data
Provided by Referees

At the time of referral to the diversion program, the intake referee was asked to fill out a questionnaire about his impressions of the youth. This "Referee Referral Form" was not used in the first two groups referred to the ADP, so the total available cases number 208. Of these, 28 were missing or had never been completed. All available forms were used in the analyses. Forms were filled out regardless of whether the youth turned out to be a control case or an experimental case. One item on the form asked the following question: "If this youth does not get into the Project, what alternative will you recommend?" The referee was given the choices of dismissal, informal-consent probation, referral to another agency, or formal handling.

Method 4—Analysis of System Processing Rates

Total processing rates for all cases handled by the juvenile court were analyzed for the four-year period preceding the start of the diversion program and for the three-year period of its operation under examination here. All cases in the population handled by the court were included in the analysis. Data were collected from official court records, which consist of monthly lists of petitions filed at the intake department. These were kept by the intake supervisor and marked with the preliminary hearing disposition. Proportions of cases processed by the court in each dispositional category were computed both monthly and yearly.

In addition, the results of a time-series analysis of the data will be presented. Using the Box and Jenkins (1976) approach, the analysis checks for shifts in trend or drift of the data and tests for any significant change in the level of the dependent variable as a result of the intervention. The intervention impact segment of the analysis is based on computer analysis techniques derived by Glass et al. (1975). The time-series analysis investigates correlational patterns in the data over time that may not be apparent by visual inspection of the graphed data.

RESULTS

Method 1

The analysis of control group dispositions showed that only a quarter (25%) of these control cases were sent on to formal handling by the court. About 37% were released outright from court jurisdiction, which indicates that these cases were in no jeopardy of deeper system involvement. While another 38% received informal probation, this typically involves little court intervention.

Were the control group dispositions valid as reference points for the typical diversion program referral case? One validity problem with this method is that the number of cases was very small, about one-fourth of the total. Also, the referee may have given a lighter disposition to the youth who was not accepted into the diversion program service component to avoid penalizing the youth for a random event.

Method 2

The classification of ADP cases by the discriminant analysis showed that most project referrals (57%) were similar to court cases that were given informal probation or adjourned for 30 days. In contrast to the control group dispositions, only about 17% were classified as similar to dismissed cases. About the same amount, 27%, fit the characteristics of formally processed cases.

Was the discriminant analysis a valid method for distinguishing the dispositional groupings of cases and classifying ADP youths accordingly? All of the evidence seems to support an affirmative answer. The variables entering the functions accounted for about 67% of the variance. The between-groups F statistics were all significant at the $p = .001$ level, indicating that the three types of dispositions involved highly distinguishable types of cases. In addition, the discriminant functions correctly classified 76% of the cases from which they were derived.

The variables that distinguished the three categories are shown in Table 3.1. Formal cases were more likely to have a not-guilty plea by the youth at the hearing than either of the dismissed or adjourned cases. Formal cases were also more likely to have had negative comments made by their parents at the hearing, but adjourned cases had more negative parent comments than dismissed cases. Formal cases were much more likely to have had a prior court record than either dismissed or adjourned cases. Adjourned cases were more likely to have been petitioned by the police than the other cases, however. Formals and adjourned cases tended to be about a year older than dismissed cases (average of 14.6 years versus 13.7). Adjourned cases more typically involved a family situation where the youth was living with the two natural parents, while the formal cases were the least likely to show this pattern.

Diversion cases usually fit the characteristics of the adjourned cases, as indicated by the discriminant analysis classifications. In Table 3.1, the ADP cases are compared with the others on the important distinguishing variables. A few discrepancies appear that prevent all of the ADP cases from being classified as similar to the typical adjourned case. In brief, ADP cases seem similar to the adjourned cases except that they had the most negative comments by parents at the hearings, were slightly more likely to have had a prior court record, were more similar to formal cases in their living situation, and occupied a middle ground in terms of age.

Method 3

In the analysis of referee questionnaire data, ADP cases once more were viewed as similar to the informal probation-adjourned category of cases. Referees recommended this as the preferred alternative disposition for 58% of their ADP referrals. In contrast to the other methods, a somewhat higher percentage (33%) was found by the referees to be fit for formal handling. Only about 8% were recommended for dismissal if they were not accepted into the diversion program. This percentage was much lower than the 17% classified as similar to dismissed cases by the discriminant analysis and the 37% dismissed by intake referees after becoming ADP control group cases.

The Referee Referral Form data are subject to at least one threat to validity, however. The fact that these forms were reviewed by diversion project staff may have produced some demand characteristics in the referees' responses. The referees may have answered the questionnaire with responses they thought would be desired or expected by the ADP staff. Another problem with the form is the use of the "informal probation" category, which was found to take the form of "adjourned for 30 days" in actual practice. It is not clear whether the referees had something different in mind for ADP cases than the procedures usually followed for a 30-day adjournment. The referees may have planned a more intensive investigation or supervision than normally used. Results of the first three methods are summarized in Table 3.2.

Method 4

If the ADP had diverted only cases that otherwise would have received formal handling, the overall rate of cases handled formally by the court would have been expected to have decreased after the initiation of the project. As indicated by the other analysis methods, however, the percentage of formal

TABLE 3.1   Major Variables Entering Discriminant Functions

Variables	Standardized Disc. Func. Coefficients	Group Means			
		Dismissed	Adjourned	(ADP)	Formal
Function 1					
Plea at hearing	-.641	1.9	1.89	1.99	1.60
Parent's comments	-.351	2.57	2.15	1.58	1.75
Recency of prior petition	.349	.13	.18	.49	1.37
Police as petitioner	-.334	.67	.76	.77	.69
Canonical discriminant function (1) at group centroids:		-1.458	-.998	—	1.207
Function 2					
Parent's comments	-.737	2.57	2.15	1.58	1.75
Age	.517	13.73	14.59	14.21	14.62
Living situation	-.503	1.65	1.52	1.70	1.85
Father present at hearing	-.386	1.43	1.36	1.46	1.31
Status offense or not	-.383	.20	.15	.14	.24
Store as petitioner	-.379	.23	.14	.13	.06
Person offense or not	-.368	.12	.05	.05	.17
Parent on youth's attitude	-.301	1.63	1.85	1.77	2.22
Canonical discriminant function (2) at group centroids:		-.582	.640	—	-.057

NOTE: Overall Wilks lambda = .334. Function 1 accounted for 88.8% of the total variance accounted for by the 2 functions. Inclusion criterion for variables in this table was a standardized canonical discriminant function coefficient over .300.

TABLE 3.2   Classifications of ADP Cases by Methods 1, 2, and 3

Method	Dismissed	*Dispositions* Informal Prob. or Adjourned	Formal Handling	Totals	(Missing)
1. Control group dispositions	22 36.7%	23 38.3%	15 25.0%	60	(2)
2. Discriminant analysis	41 16.5%	141 56.9%	66 26.6%	248	(20)
3. Referees' alt. dispositions	15 8.3%	105 58.3%	60 33.3%	180	(28)

cases in the program was probably no more than 25%-33%. With these results, there should not have been much impact on the overall system processing rates of the court.

The pre-post change in percentage of cases formally processed was indeed minimal. The court population rates of formally handled cases dropped from 57% to 53%, a nonsignificant difference. Analysis of the random sample of archival court data produced the same finding, with a 56% to 54% pre-post change. Controlling for a policy change that sharply reduced the number of status offenders handled by the court while the project was going on, the number of formally processed cases actually increased from 45% to 50%. However, this was also a nonsignificant difference.

The time-series analysis used verified data from the random sample of archival court data due to some record-keeping discrepancies found in the monthly lists kept for the total population of cases. Both the pre-ADP and post-ADP data plots were best described by the time series ARIMA (0,0,0) model—essentially a "white-noise" model indicating little change in trend or drift. The graph of the autocorrelation function showed that the series did not predict itself; there were near-zero, nonsignificant correlations between all lags of data. The effect of the diversion program as an intervention was assessed by t-tests of significance on independent samples. For all cases, and for nonstatus cases handled separately, the t-tests were not significant.

The impact on the overall court figures most likely would have not been large even if all of the ADP cases were drawn from those in jeopardy of formal processing. The total amount of ADP cases was 268, which was only 10% of the court's caseload at intake. Given the findings that only about one-fourth of these were formals, the lack of impact is not surprising.

DISCUSSION

Were the goals of diversion carried out during the first three years of the Adolescent Diversion Project? Did the project have the effect of widening the net of social control by involving youths who would not otherwise have penetrated the court system? It seems clear that the project did not divert substantial numbers of cases in jeopardy of formal handling and therefore possible formal probation or institutionalization. The project did not achieve the goal of reducing the court's formal caseload. Most of the diversion referrals were diverted from the state of limbo known as the 30-day adjournment. This can sometimes involve supervision and monitoring of behavior by an intake referee or a student intern. It can sometimes involve some rules of informal probation that the youth must follow. It can also involve merely a rescheduling of the intake hearing with no court contact in the interim. Immediate referral to the diversion program probably lessened the amount of court contact most of these cases would have received had they been on informal probation or 30-day adjournment. The ADP was certainly a more intrusive experience, however, because of the one-to-one contact with a volunteer for 6-8 hours per week for 18 weeks.

Evaluation of the project's success is dependent on the degree of success expected, as well as on one's definition of diversion. Given that most diversion programs studied to date have similar or worse records of net-widening (Saul, 1981), the ADP may at least be holding its own. And if diversion means alternative service provision away from the court for young people in some need of help, then perhaps the ADP fulfilled this model of intervention. But if diversion means removing from the court jurisdiction those who are in distinct jeopardy of traditional formal court handling, then the ADP cannot be said to have completely fulfilled the terms of this model.

Explanations for Net-Widening

How do diversion programs end up serving the wrong set of clients? The reasons seem to be tied closely to the organizational goals and resources of the court system. In the ADP, and in other programs, a large percentage of the cases appear similar to those that otherwise would have been adjourned for 30 days or put on informal probation. As mentioned earlier, this type of case receives only minimal treatment by the court. They are perceived by court personnel as needing some sort of services, yet they do not warrant formal probation or institutional services. Diversion programs with services provide a ready alternative for these cases. Services are provided but with little court involvement. The court then has an outlet for these cases, and fills its quotas of diversion referrals with them, leaving less room for the formal cases. The court feels it has helped the juveniles by providing services and can justify the referrals by the prevention philosophy of service provision (see Blomberg, 1980; Bullington et al., 1976; Klein, 1979; Sarri and Bradley, 1980).

Under this philosophy, it is better to be safe than sorry—not unlike the situations in which criminal justice officials are involved in predictions of dangerousness. There is less risk in predicting a false positive—predicting someone to be violent who turns out not to be—than in predicting a false negative, where a violent person is sent free (Monahan, 1981).Thus, the relative levels of risk in prediction contribute to the practice of providing services or treatment in cases where there is some uncertainty. By widening the net of service over more people, the agency can maximize its chances of catching the true positives—the criminals who would go on to commit violent criminal acts.

Hence, the court tries to *expand* the number of youngsters receiving some kind of services rather than reduce it. Diverting a juvenile who would otherwise receive formal probation services could thus be construed as a wasted opportunity to provide diversion services to a youth who would otherwise have to be dismissed.

Another explanation is related to this directly but centers on the court's use of its available resources. In this sense, the court has a usually fixed amount of resources that it can devote to service provision. Diversion programs often have been funded externally and can thus be considered supplemental to the regular court programs. Court officials may thus view diversion programs as opportunities for additional service provision, rather than as alternatives to their traditional services. The court's penchant for self-perpetuation, typical of most bureaucratic organizations, prevents it from dismantling its formal probation caseload by diverting these cases (see Blomberg, 1977; Pabon, 1978; Rappaport et al., 1979). Instead, the court maintains the same level of formally handled cases and expands the number of cases receiving services by referring less serious cases to diversion.

Prevention of Net-Widening

Currently, diversion programs depend on the cooperation of court officials to receive referrals. Diversion advocates wishing to prevent net-widening must either gain more control over the referral process or persuade court officials to refer the right kinds of cases. The organizational forces in the court operating to produce net-widening appear too strong to be overcome by mere persuasion, however. Why expect law enforcement and justice system workers to cooperate fully with a program this is basically antagonistic to their traditional operations? Diversion programs were developed from the rationale that traditional court and police handling of delinquents was ineffective and harmful and should be reduced or even destroyed. The stakes are too high to expect acquiescence to the reformist goals of diversion—jobs, funding, status, and organizational survival lie in the balance (Rappaport et al., 1979).

Diversion program advocates need to make administrative agreements with court officials that are directed by a higher agency or legislature and that give less discretionary power to court referees. These agreements should provide strict referral guidelines based on empirically derived profiles of the kinds of cases to be eligible for diversion referral. In brief, the profiles would be developed from an archival study of court decision-making in the particular district, focusing on the characteristics of cases sent on to formal handling. Specific ranges could be given for key variables predictive of formal handling. At the time of each referral, the program staff person would check the case against the guidelines and determine the appropriateness of the referral. Continual monitoring would thus be built into the referral process, and diversion staff would be free to reject a case if it was not appropriate. The initial agreement, of course, would also have to indicate the number of referrals to be made each year to ensure receiving enough cases.

Another method of changing the way the court uses diversion programs would be to set up diversion *without* services. The court then would not be able to view the program in terms of supplemental service provision. The rarity of this kind of true diversion is testimony to the truth of the proposition that courts wish to employ diversion program services for their own purposes.

CONCLUSIONS

Diversion programs as now operated are of ambiguous value. As seen in this study and others, the risk of widening the net of social control over an expanded range of youths is high. The benefits to these juveniles of diversion services may not outweigh the risk of reinvolvement in the justice system. This question brings other evaluative criteria into the examination of diversion programs. For example, does the program tend to bring the juveniles into more contact with law enforcement agents? Does the program "encapsulate" the juveniles into an alternate service system—trading the delinquent label for the socially handicapped label? Does the program provide skills and opportunities for the youths to help avoid future legal trouble?

Some diversion programs, such as the Adolescent Diversion Project, are specifically geared toward avoiding justice system involvement and providing empowerment skills to the juveniles. In these terms, the program is probably not harmful to its clients—in fact, it may be quite beneficial. However, by allowing referral of cases not targeted for diversion, the program may still fail to help the very people for which it was created. In addition, it will fail to produce radical change in the court system by failing to remove any substantial number of cases from traditional formal court handling.

At this point, the future of diversion looks bleak. External funding, traditionally provided by the federal government, is drying up, leaving diversion programs even more at the mercy of local justice system agencies. Those agencies that do decide to pick up the tab for continuation of diversion programming will likely demand even more control over the programs. This would likely reach the point where diversion programs become just another component of traditional court services.

FUTURE RESEARCH

Given the importance of organizational variables to court decision-making and diversion referrals, they warrant closer investigation in future studies. Future research should also test the success of programs that experiment with alternative diversion referral procedures and agreements. Also, diversion without services should be compared with the usual programs, if the necessary agreements can be established.

One of the major purposes of this study has been to develop and employ better evaluative strategies for testing the types of cases referred to diversion programs. Research should proceed from this development to ensure adequate program evaluation The multimethod evaluation system utilized here has proven useful and is recommended for future studies. Explicit evaluation of the organizational and system-level impacts of diversion will help us to initiate social interventions that achieve their goals.

REFERENCES

BLOMBERG, T. (1980) "Widening the net: an anomaly in the evaluation of diversion programs," pp. 572-592 in M. Klein and K. Teilmann (eds.) Handbook of Criminal Justice Evaluation. Beverly Hills, CA: Sage.

——— (1977) "Diversion and accelerated social control." Journal of Criminal Law and Criminology 68: 274-282.

BOX, G. E. P. and G. M. JENKINS (1976) Time-Series Analysis: Forecasting and Control. San Francisco: Holden-Day.

BULLINGTON, B., J. SPROWLS, D. KATKIN, and M. PHILLIPS (1978) "A critique of diversionary juvenile justice." Crime and Delinquency 24: 59-71.

CAPLAN, N. and S. D. NELSON (1973) "On being useful: the nature and consequences of psychological research on social problems." American Psychologist 28: 199-211.

CRESSEY, D. R. and R.A. McDERMOTT (1973) Diversion from the Juvenile Justice System. Ann Arbor: National Assessment of Juvenile Corrections, University of Michigan.

GAYLIN, W., I. GLASSER, S. MARCUS, and D. ROTHMAN (1978) Doing Good: The Limits of Benevolence. New York: Pantheon.

GIBBONS, D. C. and G. F. BLAKE (1976) "Evaluating the impact of juvenile diversion programs." Crime and Delinquency 22: 411-420.

GLASS, G. V., V. L. WILLSON, and J. M. GOTTMAN (1975) Design and Analysis of Time-Series Experiments. Boulder: Colorado Associated University Press.

GOLD, M. and J. R. WILLIAMS (1969) "The effects of getting caught: apprehension of the juvenile offender as a cause of subsequent delinquencies." Prospectus: A Journal of Law Reform 3: 1-12.

HOWLETT, F. W. (1973) "Is the YSB all it's cracked up to be?" Crime and Delinquency 19: 485-492.

In re GAULT (1967) 387 U.S. 1

JAMES, H. (1969) Children in Trouble: A National Scandal. New York: Christian Science Monitor Publishers.

KLAPMUTS, N. (1974) "Diversion from the justice system." Crime and Delinquency 6: 108-131.

KLEIN, M. (1979) "Deinstitutionalization and diversion of juvenile offenders: a litany of impediments," in N. Morris and M. Tonry (eds.) Crime and Justice: An Annual Review of Research, Vol. 1. Chicago: University of Chicago Press.

——— K. S. TEILMANN, S. B. LINCOLN, and S. LABIN (1979) Diversion as Operationalization of Labeling Theory. Final report on Project No. MH26147 to the Center for Studies in Crime and Delinquency, National Institute of Mental Health. Los Angeles: Social Science Research Institute, University of Southern California.

MONAHAN, J. (1981) Predicting Violent Behavior: An Assessment of Clinical Techniques. Beverly Hills, CA: Sage.

NEJELSKI, P. (1976) "Diversion: the promise and the danger." Crime and Delinquency 22: 393-41.

PABON, E. (1978) "Changes in juvenile justice: evolution or reform." Social Work 23: 492-497.

PALMER, T. and R. LEWIS (1980) An Evaluation of Juvenile Diversion. Cambridge, MA: Oelgeschlager, Gunn, & Hain.

RAPPAPORT, J. (1981) "In praise of paradox: a social policy of empowerment over prevention." American Journal of Community Psychology 9.

——— E. SEIDMAN, and W. S. DAVIDSON (1979) "Demonstration research and manifest versus true adoption: the natural history of a research project to divert adolescents from the legal system," pp. 101-104 in R. F. Munoz et al. (eds.) Social and Psychological Research in Community Settings: Designing and Conducting Programs for Social and Personal Well-Being. San Francisco: Jossey-Bass.

RUTHERFORD, A. and R. McDERMOTT (1976) Juvenile Diversion. Washington, DC: National Institute of Law Enforcement and Criminal Justice, LEAA.

SARRI, R. and P. W. BRADLEY (1980) "Juvenile aid panels: an alternative to juvenile court processing in South Australia." Crime and Delinquency 26: 42-62.

SAUL, J. A. (1981) "Do juvenile diversion programs widen the net of social control? An application of system-level evaluation strategies." Master's thesis, Michigan State University.

SEIDMAN, E. (1980) "The route from the successful experiment to policy formation: falling rocks, bumps and dangerous curves." Presented at the annual meeting of the American Society of Criminology, San Francisco, November.

U.S. President's Commission on Law Enforcement and the Administration of Justice (1967) The Challenge of Crime in a Free Society. Washington, DC: Government Printing Office.
WRESINSKI, M. D., J. A. SAUL, D. I. BYBEE, W. S. DAVIDSON, and J. R. KOCH (1980) "Prevention of juvenile delinquency: evaluating the systems impact of diversion." Presented at the 88th Annual Convention of the American Psychological Association, Montreal.

Merry Morash

Michigan State University

4

TWO MODELS OF COMMUNITY CORRECTIONS
One for the Ideal World,
One for the Real World

This chapter summarizes a number of findings from a study of adolescents' involvement in community programs in two parts of Boston. Because the study was conducted in 1979 and 1980, after most of the juvenile correctional institutions in Massachusetts had been closed, the adolescents who were studied included the majority of youths with police and court involvement, as well as a small proportion (16.7%) of the 54 youths who had been referred to the state correctional agency, the Massachusetts Division of Youth Services (MDYS), during the year. It therefore was possible to examine the quantity and quality of participation in community programs by youths who varied considerably in official and unofficial delinquency. The analysis of adolescents' involvement with community programs—including schools, employment programs, counsel-seling programs, recreational programs, and health programs—served as the empirical basis for drawing conclusions about the feasibility of relying on the integration (or reintegration) of adolescent offenders into existing community programs as a method for correcting delinquent behavior.

It should be noted that the focus of the research was not on specifically correctional programs, which may or may not be located in the community, but rather on the network of programs that are considered to constitute part of the legitimate community. Correctional programs are considered only if they are

AUTHOR'S NOTE: Data were collected for this study under grant 78-JN-AX-0018 from the National Institute for Juvenile Justice and Delinquency Prevention, Law Enforcement Assistance Administration. The sponsoring agency for the data collection was Blackstone Institute. I would like to thank William Oshima, Francis Rowan, and Bozenna Buda for their assistance in collecting the data. I am solely responsible for the contents of this chapter.

actually in the community where the youth normally lives but not if they are in some other community.

Social control theory, as developed by Hirschi (1969), Hindelang (1973), and Hepburn (1976), is a key theoretical basis for the contention that the development of ties between offenders and the legitimate elements of their own communities contributes to lawful behavior. The key proposition of social control theory is that attachment to other people who represent a nondelinquent lifestyle, commitment to conventional behaviors, involvement in time-consuming legal activities, and attitudes toward conformity result in lawful behavior. Thus, along with family and friends, community groups and organizations can play a part in reducing delinquency by providing attachments to staff and to peers who are engaged in nondelinquent pursuits, and by filling the time available for delinquent activity. Put another way, the network of community programs for adolescents can curb delinquency to the extent that it provides meaningful and legitimate interactions and roles for youths (Shichor, 1980: 327).

Although community programs for adolescents hypothetically can affect delinquency, it is not at all clear that they can accomplish this in reality. By surveying a number of youths in two urban communities where, due to state policy, only a very small number of delinquents had been placed outside the community, we developed a profile of youths' interactions with community programs and of their experiences in these programs. The survey results revealed that there are serious questions about relying on existing networks of community programs to prevent and treat delinquency, at least in the types of communities where the study was conducted. First, the majority of programs available are recreational facilities that, relative to other types of programs, have characteristics that are less conducive to the development of a strong bond to the legitimate community. Second, schools in particular seem to be inadequate settings for developing such a bond, particularly for the delinquent youths who are the target population of correctional efforts.

METHODOLOGY

Study Setting

The study was conducted in two different types of urban communities, both of which are located in the city of Boston. The first community exemplifies a *communal* community (Spergel, 1976). Residents are primarily white and working class, and the community is characterized by strong ethnic (Italian), kinship, and primary group ties. Population mobility is low, and the community is geographically separated from the rest of the city by ocean channels that make make it necessary to use either a tunnel or bridges to reach it.

The second community is best described as a mix between a *pluralistic* and *disorganized* community. It contains a mixture of racial and ethnic groups, with a majority of the residents being white but a relatively large minority being black. There is also a diversity of social classes, due in part to the movement of middle-class families back into the inner city. The community is physically fragmented, with a turnpike dividing it. Unplanned development has resulted in a confusing conglomeration of deteriorating industrial plants and warehouses mingled with small shops and residential areas, some of which include concentrations of destitute families. The population mobility is moderate to high, ranging from 37% to 52% in the three census tract areas. Reflecting the heterogeneity of the area, nearly one-quarter of the families are poor, with incomes under $5,000, whereas one-third of the working population have professional-level jobs.

Sample

A sample of 1073 youths was drawn from school, police, court, and MDYS records in the two communities. For a selected year, all youths with police, court, and MDYS contact were included, and a systematic sample of public school students was taken. Fortunately for the present study, the school records did include the names of some dropouts, and although dropouts without juvenile records still may have been underrepresented, they were not omitted. If youths had a record of a more serious contact with the juvenile justice system than was reflected by the category in which they were initially sampled, they were reclassified to the more serious subgroup.

All the subjects were mailed an invitation to be in the study, and just under 15% returned an answer by mail. For the remaining youths, considerable effort was made to establish telephone and/or personal contact. Personal contact included visits to the youth's home, school and/or street corner. The use of each of these approaches when the more easily accomplished had failed left us with 146 youths who could not be reached by any means. Of the 927 who were contacted, 63.4% (n = 588) eventually participated in a one- to three-hour interview and received a payment of $10. The proportion of youths contacted who participated was 61.8% (n = 362) for those in the school group, 69.5% (n = 116) for the police group, and 68.7% (n = 101) for the court group. Only 16.7% (n = 9) of the 54 youths with an MDYS record participated in the research. In cases of nonparticipation in the MDYS group, the youth had been removed from the community and contact with community programs, and therefore an interview could not be arranged.

Structure of the Survey Instrument and Measurement

The study participants were asked to name all of the community programs they had attended during the last year, including school. In order to improve recall, initial responses to the question were followed by a display listing all known programs in the community where the youth resided. Detailed information was collected on the experiences of youths in each of the programs. Youths also were asked to provide information about themselves and their families. Short telephone interviews with a parent and juvenile records provided additional information (e.g., social class) on each youth. Thus, the survey generated information on each subject and on all programs the subjects attended.

A measure of the self-reported delinquency of the subjects was obtained with an adaptation of Gold's (1970) scale, which reflects both the frequency and seriousness of delinquency. The adaptation eliminated all items referring to status offenses. The Hollingshead-Redlich scale (described by Myers and Roberts, 1959) was used to measure social class. Because blacks were the predominant minority group in both areas and white youths represented the majority group, dummy variable coding was used, and black youths were assigned the score of 1, while white youths made up the residual category.

In order to indicate the experiences of youths in the programs, Moos's (1975) scales for community programs were used to measure youths' perceptions of each program they said they attended in the last year. Moos's scales focus on nine dimensions of program climate:

(1) Participants are *involved* in the day-to-day functioning of the program.
(2) Participants are encouraged to be helpful and *supportive* toward other participants, and staff are *supportive* of participants.
(3) The program encouraged the open *expression of feelings.*
(4) Participants are encouraged to be *autonomous* by taking initiative in planning activities and by taking leadership.
(5) The participant is *oriented toward practical considerations* such as job training.
(6) Participants are *oriented to personal problems* and feelings and to seek to understand them.
(7) *Order and organization* are stressed in the program.
(8) There is *clarity* about participants' expectations regarding the day-to-day routine of program rules and procedures.
(9) Staff use regulations to keep participants *under control.*

Another scale was used to measure perceived dimensions of interpersonal relations between youths and staffs. Wish et al. (1976) had previously used factor analysis to identify the dimensions of role relationships between people. Their factor analysis was repeated for the present research and it yielded three of the original four factors, one of which included elements of two of the factors identified by Wish et al. In the present analysis, the three dimensions of role relationships were (1) competitive and hostile versus cooperative and friendly; (2) task-oriented, formal. and superficial versus emotional, informal, and intense; and (3) unequal versus equal.

Five other indexes were constructed specifically for use in the present research. To establish the youths' perceptions of the stigmatization of participants in the community programs they attended, they were asked the following question about each program: "Do you think that the kids who come to this program are like typical neighborhood kids?" Following affirmative responses, the youths were asked to describe the differences they perceived. Youths could describe up to two differences, and the differences described were later categorized.

The second index that was constructed consisted of responses to questions about the extent to which each program assisted the youth in participating in other community programs. The score for this scale was a function of the number of community programs, employment opportunities, and the educational opportunities to which staff had provided a referral or for which staff had provided assistance in establishing a positive interaction (e.g., help doing well in school). This index was used to reflect the degree to which programs contributed to the development of linkage between their participants and other community resources.

The third index indicated exposure to delinquency and was based on reports of exposure to illegal activities by other program participants while they were involved in program activities.

For the fourth index, responses to questions about the use and sale of marijuana and other illegal drugs were used to construct an 8-point indicator of drug-related delinquency, which is a type of delinquency not considered in the Gold scale.

The fifth index constructed reflected the number and importance of the activities in which youths took part when they attended each program.

Finally, open-ended questions were used to collect information about the things youths disliked about the programs that they knew of and that they attended; and for the programs they attended, the nature of their activities in the program. Responses were later categorized.

FINDINGS

Types of Programs Available

Most (66%) of the 588 youths who were surveyed reported having contact with one or two programs, including school programs, during the last year (see Table 4.1). Just under 20% said they had contact with three programs. At the extremes, 6% said they were not in contact with any community programs during the year, and 8% had taken part in four, five, and even six different programs.

Programs were classified as one of nine types: recreation and sports, helping and oriented toward solving personal and/or family problems, health (not

TABLE 4.1   Proportion of Youths Using Nine Types
              of Programs (percentages)

Type of Program	Proportion of Youths Reporting Use	Number of Different Programs of this Type Used			
		1	2	3	4
Recreation and sports	49.1	34.0	13.0	2.0	0.1
Help	3.1	2.8	.3		
Health	6.0	6.0			
Job	15.6	15.0	.6		
Teen center	10.0	10.0			
Outreach	4.0	4.0			
Social control	4.6	4.6			
School	89.8	89.8			
Other	7.7	7.7			

including private physicians), job training and employment, teen centers, streetwork, correctional, school, and other. Other programs were those that were attended by only a few of our subjects, and they included such things as a historical association and the Kiwanis Key Club. The classification scheme was based on all of the organizations and groups respondents had attended in the communities where the study was conducted.

Although most youths took part in a school program, and just under half were in a recreational program, other services affected very small proportions of the youths (Table 4.1). This is important to keep in mind, for although the study is focused on youths' involvement in community programs, it is clear that the majority of youths have no contacts with programs besides school and those that are recreational.

Programs Other than Schools

Comparisons were made between all of the categories of community programs (except for schools), which, due to their importance as a socialization institution for adolescents, were considered separately. When ANOVA procedures were used (not shown) to test for differences between youths' perceptions of the nonschool programs, three patterns were apparent. The usually large recreational centers, which were the type of nonschool program attended by the largest number of youths, were characterized by their failure relative to other community programs to provide practical or personal help to youths, or to involve youths in positive attachments to staff (see Table 4.2). A second type of program, the employment and helping programs, and the settlement program, were differentiated by their provision of more help with practical and/or personal problems, and more positive relationships to staff (Table 4.3). An

TABLE 4.2   Youths' Experiences in 7 Recreational Programs

Type of Program	n	Characteristics of the Program Relative to Other Programs
Sports leagues	65	*less* perceived emphasis on personal problems, order and organization; *more* perceived involvement, frequent attendance, desire to attend, cooperative relationships with staff, intense/informal/ personal relationships with staff; *more* reported exposure to youths fighting, swearing, and being late
Gym I	51	*less* perceived orientation toward personal problems, intense/informal/personal relationships with staff, frequent attendance, exposure to rule breaking by participants; *tendency* to form no close personal relationships with any staff person
Gym II	21	*less* perceived support, practical orientation, order and organization, clarity about rules, cooperative relationships with staff; *more* reported use of expulsion from the program to maintain order
Boys Club I	71	*less* reported emphasis on linkage to other programs; *more* perceived involvement, emphasis on order and organization
Boys Club II	20	no differences from averages for other programs
Community school I	82	*less* perceived support, expressiveness, practical orientation, personal problem orientation, clarity about rules, frequent participation, informal/intense/personal relationships with staff, emphasis on linkage to other programs; *more* perceived use of expulsion as a punishment, exposure to other youths using drugs, assaulting youths and staff, stealing, selling drugs; *tendency* to form no close personal relationships with any staff person
Community school II	55	*less* perceived support, expressiveness, practical orientation, frequent involvement, emphasis on linkage to other programs

overall finding is that with the exception of the settlement house, the programs in which the youths perceived the more positive climate and relationships with staff served quite small numbers of the youths whom we interviewed.

TABLE 4.3   Youths' Experiences in Helping, Settlement, and Correctional Programs

Type of Program	n	Characteristics of the Program Relative to Other Programs
Mental health	11	*more* expressiveness, practical orientation, emphasis on order and organization
Settlement house	77	*more* expressiveness, autonomy, practical problem orientation, clarity about rules, informal/intense/personal relations with staff
Streetwork programs	22	*more* involvement, expressiveness, autonomy, practical orientation, personal problem orientation, cooperative relationships with staff, emphasis on linkage to other community programs
Church programs	46	*less* frequent attendance, emphasis on linkage to other programs; *more* involvement, support, autonomy, order and organization
Antipoverty program I	33	*less* clarity about rules; *more* practical orientation, frequent attendance
Antipoverty program II	87	*less* perceived involvement, autonomy, personal problem orientation, informal/intense/emotional relationships with staff, frequent attendance; *more* help securing a job
Probation	20	*less* involvement, clarity, frequent attendance, desire to attend, exposure to others' delinquency; *more* social control, formal/superficial/task-oriented relationships with staff, help locating jobs
State corrections (MDYS)	7	*more* hostile relationships with staff, frequent attendance, emphasis on linkage to other programs.

The third program category that stood out as different from the others was the local court probation program. Youths perceived their participation in the probation programs to be characterized by more negative experiences in comparison to other programs. However, few youths were involved in an active program of probation counseling.

Focusing first on the recreational centers, which were the programs attended by the greatest number of subjects (with the exception of sports leagues), common characteristics were relatively negative relationships between participants and staff, little attention to individuals' feelings and personal problems, few attempts to help youths link up with other community programs, and, in some cases, a total absence of interaction between program participants and staff. An absence of interaction occurred when youths used gym or swimming facilities but did not become involved with staff. Two of the six recreational centers relied heavily on expelling youths as a method of maintaining order. Specifically, 44% of the 21 youths interviewed in one program had been expelled at some time during the last year, and 26% of the 82 interviewed in another program had been expelled. On the whole what goes on in the large recreational centers—gyms, community school after-school programs, and boys clubs—seems to be antithetical to the development of attachment to staff, personal involvement, and meaningful roles that are required by a community correctional approach as we have defined it.

One type of recreational program was an exception—the sports leagues. They were characterized by relatively high levels of involvement, positive relations with staff, and frequent and willing attendance. The leagues were structured differently from the other recreational programs, for they were not primarily providing (and protecting) a facility for a large number of youthful users. Instead, the leagues organized small, team-sized groups whose members were stable over time. It is likely that this difference contributes to the more positive outcomes.

In contrast to most of the recreational facilities, helping services, employment programs, streetwork programs, and church programs served proportionately fewer youths, but they provided more of the involvement and attachment that are believed to prevent and correct delinquency. The settlement house served a large proportion of the subjects, but it also tended to promote positive ties. This can be explained by the decentralized structure of the settlement house: It did not operate as one program, but rather had four neighborhood branches and three or four centralized but small programs. Except for the employment programs, the decentralized and small programs were marked by relatively more positive relationships between youths and staff, and attention to personal problems and feelings (Table 4.3). The employment program participants reported that they were taking part in the program for a long period each week, and it provided practical-oriented services.

The small number of youths reporting on their participation in probation programs indicated that in these programs they perceived relatively low levels of involvement, low levels of clarity about expectations, and high levels of social control, and that they attended many fewer days per month than participants in other programs. One-third said they would like to continue attending, which, as might be expected, is a much lower percentage than participants in other programs, where 78% wanted to continue attending. Relationships tended to be more formal, superficial, and task-oriented with the probation staff than with staff in other programs. There were indications that probationers received much more help in locating jobs than did the participants in other programs. Because the program was oriented toward individuals rather than groups, participants were much less likely to be exposed to the delinquency of other youths during their visits to the program than were clients of other agencies[1].

It is important to note that the difference in the various kinds of programs could not usually be explained as the result of proportionately more of the seriously delinquent youths attending, or of proportionately more youths of a particular race or social class attending. The only programs that served proportionately more youths who reported a high level of delinquency were the streetwork, probation, and state correctional (MDYS) programs, and just the streetwork program served proportionately more youths who reported a high level of drug-related delinquency. It is of interest that even these three programs apparently differed from each other, not because of the type of youth served, but because of program structure and content.

The general impression that the network of community programs offered predominantly recreational facilities rather than settings where youths were engaged in more demanding and involving roles was further confirmed by a survey question about the activities of the youths when they participated in each program. The 588 youths were encouraged to describe up to four activities for each of the 742 contacts they described. They described a total of 1723 different activities, which were later categorized. The vast majority (78.5%) of activities were recreational—for example, games, sports, dances, television viewing, and arts and crafts. Only 9.1% of the activities were paid or volunteer work, though an additional .5% were "looking for work." Also, a small proportion of the activities that were mentioned were study (3.4%), receiving medical or counseling help (4.9%), camping (1.3), and waiting (.3%). The only indication of anything like the "meaningful roles" that would be likely to result in a strong bond was club-type memberships to plan activites and raise money, or participation in self-government; just 2.1% of all activities mentioned were of these types.

In conclusion, an examination of youths' experiences in the networks of nonschool programs in two urban communities shows that for the most part, the preponderance of services adolescents receive from community programs involved recreational facilities. With the exception of sports leagues, the recreational facilities are comparatively more like institutions than are the smaller or decentralized programs that focus on other needs of youths; that is, they generally provided less positive interactions with staff and less positive involvement than did other programs. It is therefore doubtful that recreational facilities are well suited as settings for developing the bonds that restrain youths from delinquency.

TABLE 4.4 Comparison of Mean Scores for School and
Other Community Programs

	School Programs		Other Community Programs		
	$\bar{x}$	n	$\bar{x}$	n	t
Climate					
Involvement	2.5	525	2.9	630	5.7*
Support	2.5	525	2.7	632	2.2*
Expressiveness	2.2	525	2.3	632	1.9
Autonomy	2.2	525	2.5	630	4.2*
Practical problem orientation	2.8	518	2.2	626	10.2*
Personal problem orientation	1.3	525	1.3	630	.7
Order orientation	2.4	525	3.2	633	10.4*
Clarity about rules	2.7	525	3.0	629	4.9*
Social control orientation	2.4	525	2.3	630	.4
Linkage to other programs	1.6	526	2.3	742	7.4*
Exposure to delinquency	7.3	526	3.6	633	16.8*
Days attended/month	18.7	526	10.7	742	21.5*
Role relationship with staff					
Hostile	.03	526	−.03	562	1.2
Formal/superficial/ task-oriented	.10	526	−.09	562	3.8*
Unequal	.09	526	−.07	562	3.6*

*$p \leqslant .01$

The Schools

Schools represent the highest concentration of community program resources that are available to adolescents, and, as might be expected, a common objective of delinquency programs is to involve youths in school programs. This is a questionable practice for more than one reason.

First, compared with youths' perceptions of climate in other community programs, their perception of the climate in schools was marked by less involvement, less autonomy, less order and organization, and less clarity about rules (Table 4.4)[2]. However, participants in school programs did perceive a more practical orientation, including an orientation toward employment, than did participants in other programs. Relationships with key staff members (primarily teachers) were more formal, task-oriented, and superficial than in other programs, and they were more unequal. In response to a series of open-ended questions about their likes and dislikes about school programs, 11% of the youths said that in school they did not like the staff, and 16% volunteered that staff were not supportive (e.g., helpful, understanding). Taken together, the pattern of response suggests that schools, even more than other community programs, are unable to provide the bonds to the legitimate community that are required to control delinquency. This is a particularly serious shortcoming in light of the concentration of community resources for adolescents in the schools.

An examination of the correlations between characteristics of youths in school and the kinds of experiences they had at school shows that it is the most delinquent youths who have the more negative experiences (Table 4.5). These correlations, though, are generally weak, which shows that many youths who are not involved in serious delinquency have the negative experiences in schools. Self-reports of serious delinquency were weakly correlated with hostile relationships with school staff, superficial, formal, or task-oriented relationships, unequal relationships, lower levels of attendance and the impression that school activities are unimportant. Similarly, self-reports of drug-related delinquency were related to hostile relationships with key school staff and to low levels of attendance. There also were moderate correlations of both drug-related and other delinquency to exposure to other school students who were breaking the law while they were taking part in the school program. The correlations show that particularly for youths who self-report high levels of delinquency, schools are not likely to fill their time or to provide the setting for attachments to teachers. They are, though, settings where the more serious delinquents come together and are exposed to each others' delinquent activity.

The exclusion of youths from school, as indicated by their status as dropouts or by their temporary suspension, is further evidence that the school setting is not particularly conducive to the formation of bonds between at least some subgroups of adolescents and the legitimate community institutions. Youths who did not attend school self-reported greater delinquency, greater drug-related delinquency, and deeper penetration into the juvenile justice system (Table 4.6). Attendance was unrelated, however, to social class, race, or sex. In similar pattern, males, youths who were high in drug-related and other self-reported delinquency, and youths who were most involved with the juvenile justice system were more likely to have been expelled from school (Table 4.7). As with attendance, social class and race were unrelated to being expelled.

DISCUSSION

Depending on one's orientation toward either an ideal or a real-world view of the network of community programs, the process of integrating delinquent youths into community programs where they develop bonds to the legitimate

TABLE 4.5 Correlations of Characteristics of Youths with Their Experiences in School (n = 526)

Experiences	Delinquency	Delinquency (Drugs)	Penetration	Social Class	Female	Black	Communal Community
Relations with staff							
Hostile	.13*	.09*	.03	.11*	.04	-.08**	
Superficial/formal	.07**	.05	.11*	-.11*	-.02	-.11*	
Unequal	.13*	.05	.07**	.07**	-.13	-.01	
Linkage to other programs	-.03	-.02	-.03	.06	.06	.12	
Exposure to delinquency	.30*	.30*	.01	-.03	.15*	-.02	
Days attended	-.18*	-.20*	-.12*	-.04	-.05	-.00	
Importance of school	-.11*	-.06	-.21*	.03	.18*	.02	

*p ≤ .01
**p ≤ .05

TABLE 4.6   Comparison of Youths Who Do and Who Do Not
             Attend School

| | Attendance | | |
	Yes ($n = 526$)	No ($n = 57$)	t
Comparison of means			
Seriousness of delinquency	3.8	5.5	2.4*
Drug-related delinquency	1.6	2.6	3.2**
Penetration	1.5	2.3	6.8**
Social class (low score = higher class)	55.7	57.0	.8
Comparison of proportions			χ^2
Male	88.5%	11.5%	
Female	92.8%	7.2%	2.4
White	89.4%	10.6%	
Black	95.9%	4.1%	2.3

*$p \leqslant .05$
**$p \leqslant .01$

society can be viewed in two ways. At one extreme, based on the ideal world view, it is a relatively unhindered process of referring youths to existing programs. At the other extreme, in some real communities, such as those where the present study was conducted, the process must be viewed as one of overcomming numerous obstacles to linking youths to some meaningful programs. This second view takes into account the predominantly institutional quality of the networks of community programs in the two areas studied. A contrast of the ideal and the real experiences of adolescents as they interact with community programs suggests three common errors in our thinking about community corrections as a process for linking youths to the legitimate elements in their communities.

The first error stems from a tendency to ignore theories of delinquency when we formulate strategies for its control. As a result, it is often assumed that living in one's community and attending school are correctional experiences for delinquents. This assumption is contradicted by recent theoretical work that identifies as a cause of delinquency the failure of society in general to provide meaningful roles for adolescents (Shichor, 1980: 327), and thus a widespread lack of social bonds between adolescents and legitimate elements in our society. The assumption is contradicted, furthermore, by the social disorganization theories, which since the 1930s have pointed to the failure of highly disorganized communities in particular to meet the needs of adolescents. As Kornhauser (1978: 81) concluded from her review of these theories,

TABLE 4.7   Comparison of Youths Who Have and Have Not
Been Suspended from School

| | Suspension | | |
	Yes (n = 115)	No (n = 411)	t
Comparison of means			
Seriousness of delinquency	6.4	3.1	6.7*
Drug-related delinquency	2.8	1.3	7.1*
Penetration	1.8	1.4	5.4*
Social class (low score = higher class)	55.8	55.2	.0
Comparison of proportions			χ^2
Male	28.2%	71.8%	
Female	12.8%	87.2%	16.8*
White	21.3%	78.8%	
Black	25.7%	74.3%	.5

*p $\leqslant$ .01

social institutions that are inadequate at the community level fail to promote "attachments and commitments that enmesh the child in interlocking controls," fail to provide bonds between the child and others, and, for dropouts and pushouts, even fail to provide direct supervision. Recent theory and research have identified the urban school in particular as being devoid of meaningful roles and relationships for many adolescents. For example, the Carnegie Institute described public schools as "an alienating experience for many young people [and] like a prison—albeit with open doors—for some." This statement, which is supported by others (e.g., Schwendinger and Schwendinger, 1979: 252; Kelly, 1980), underscores the error in considering schools as places where the social bonds thought to control delinquency are likely to be formed. In general, by overlooking theories that indentify community and school as the cause of delinquency, we have sometimes erroneously concluded that they can be the cure for it.

The second error in our thinking that is brought to light by a consideration of the actual network of community programs in two urban areas is in the assumption that the correctional institutions to be replaced by community corrections efforts are an anomaly among programs for youths. It is more accurate to view the large control-oriented training schools as extremes rather than exceptions in the types of programs made available to adolescents in our society. Schools and the recreational facilities are variations on the institutional theme, according to which small numbers of adult staff supervise and attempt to control large numbers of adolescents in programs that provide neither intimate staff-youth relationships nor meaningful roles for youths to fill. The anomalies are the programs that serve small numbers of youths, such as job programs, counseling programs, and streetwork programs; in these programs climate and atmosphere are relatively more conducive to the development of a positive social bond.

The third error in our thinking about community programs concerns the function and potential effect of the group homes, small institutions, and other special programs that are commonly subsumed under the heading of community corrections programs. Actually, these programs are usually not a part of the structure of the community where the delinquent and her or his family normally live (Segal and Aviran, 1976). Instead, they are supplements to or partial replacements of basic community agencies and groups that typically serve youths. They are used for youths who come to be defined as so intolerable, by virtue of their delinquent behavior and/or some other characteristics, that they must be dealt with, at least for part of the day, outside of their usual community of residence and away from other youths judged to be more tolerable. Such programs have been demonstrated to have positive effects, particularly when compared with more restrictive institutional programs (Coates et al., 1978). Yet they replace the resident's own community for only a limited amount of time. Once services are terminated, links can be tenuous or nonexistent with the legitimate network of community programs where the youth resides. This in no way deprecates the importance of these programs as alternative to large reform schools, but it does imply that such programs can have only a limited effect, for often they will not be able to overcome the lack of a social bond between a youth and her or his own community for any but a short length of time. The term "therapeutic community" accurately reflects the function of many specialized community correctional programs, for it conveys the idea that the program replaces the participant's actual community; however, when the youth leaves the therapeutic community, the setting for developing and maintaining social bonds again is often lacking.

Before consideration is given to the practical implications of recognizing the errors in thinking that are outlined above, it is important to make two points about the interpretation of study findings. First, in considering the results of the present research, it is essential to recognize the types of communities where the data were collected. These communities did represent typical types of urban communities (Spergel, 1976), but they are not representative of all types. No doubt, communities that are more highly disorganized would have even less capacity for reintegrating youths into a potentially correctional network of services, whereas more prosperous communities with more prosperous families would have a greater capacity. The relative capacities of different types of communities to deliver services to one type of offender, the status offender, was demonstrated in recent research by Spergel et al. (1982).

In our own research, the communal community was somewhat better able than the pluralistic-disorganized one to provide positive experiences and attachments to youths (Morash and Wright, 1982). Thus, results are specific to the type of community, and they direct our attention to the importance of understanding the nature of community in any discussion of the community corrections strategy.

Second, it is necessary to consider absolute as well as comparative information on the various programs in order to reach a conclusion about the overall capacity of the network of community programs as a setting for the formation of social bonds. The comparative information is most useful in highlighting that the greatest number of youths are served by the programs that have the most negative climate and role relationships with staff and other youths. Information on the absolute number of youths who have no relationships with staff at recreational facilities; the tendency toward hostile, impersonal, formal, and unequal relationships with staff; high scores to reflect exposure to delinquency of other youths; and the high rate of suspensions and expulsions in some programs tell us that the network of community programs is unlikely to encourage the formation of bonds for many youths. In response to open-ended questions, study subjects reported that they were not usually involved in decision-making or work roles, and in the schools, relationships with staff were particularly strained. Such absolute information is most useful in showing the overall capacities of the network of community programs, which in the present research was limited insofar as encouraging social bonds was concerned.

IMPLICATIONS

The findings of this study have direct implications for the choice of strategies to correct delinquency. Although strategies of advocacy, referral, and the closing of large correctional institutions can assist some youths, for the majority and in the long run it would seem that successful efforts to correct youths within the community depend ultimately on the roles available to all adolescents in our society, and thus in part on the roles available in the network of community programs. This recognition brings us to a recurrent conclusion about delinquency treatment—that individual treatment will be overshadowed by the inadequacy of communities and the larger society to establish bonds with and meaningful roles for adolescents. In the early part of this century, Shaw and McKay (1931) as well as Thrasher (1927) reached this conclusion. Cloward and Ohlin (1960) at a later time pointed to the lack of opportunity structure available in poor communities. In the 1970s, Gemignani (1973) recommended the establishment of a comprehensive youth service network in all types of communities as a natural delinquency prevention strategy. More recently, the 1976 National Advisory Committee on Criminal Justice Standards and Goals recommended the strengthening of every part of the network of services for adolescents. At present, in the literature there is an ongoing (though not particularly widespread) attempt to explicate modern methods for strengthening the community in order to control delinquency (e.g., Sorrentino, 1977; Bute, 1981), and more generally to develop methods for engaging adolescents in meaningful roles (e.g., Pearl et al., 1978; Duggan and Shlien, 1978; Hruska, 1978). Because these strategies involve the reallocation of increasingly limited resources and/or a rethinking or beliefs about the roles adolescents can or should fill, their use depends largely on the outcome of political interchanges.

In the absence of widespread political action and change in beliefs about adolescents, three strategies for the control of delinquency are appropriate. One, which is currently the most evident, is to continue to rely on group homes, special schools, and similar programs as a temporary supplement to existing community resources for these youths who are not tolerated by the community. The second strategy is to establish alternative programs that provide new and meaningful roles to adolescents in geographically limited areas. The third strategy is, of course, a large-scale reform effort aimed at the educational and other programs available to adolescents. To the extent that social bond is a determinant of delinquency and can be developed in school, job, and other programs, the first strategy is only a temporary and limited solution, but the other two hold some promise as long-term delinquency control measures.

NOTES

1. As already noted, only a small number of youths who were involved in MDYS were interviewed. Therefore, only 7 MDYS-operated correctional programs were described. Although information on the MDYS programs can only be viewed as suggestive, tests did show that participants had significantly more hostile relationships with staff, received more help in making. linkages to other programs, and attended more days per week than did participants in other programs.

2. In Table 4.4 the number of nonschool programs varies depending on whether the youth could describe any interaction with a staff person or enough exposure to the program to be able to report on program climate.

REFERENCES

BUTE, J., Jr. (1981) "Practicing from theory: work with youths and reflections on radical criminology." Crime and Delinquency 27: 106-121.

CLOWARD, R. A. and L. E. OHLIN (1960) Delinquency and Opportunity. New York: Free Press.

COATES, R. B., A. D. MILLER, and L. E. OHLIN (1978) Diversity in a Youth Correctional System. Cambridge, MA: Ballinger.

DUGGAN, H. and J. SHLIEN (1978) "The childcare apprenticeship program: an experiment in cross-age intervention," in E. Wenk and N. Harlow (eds.) School Crime and Disruption. Davis, CA: Responsible Action.

ELLIOTT, D. S. and H. L. VOSS (1974) Delinquency and Dropout. Lexington, MA: D. C. Heath.

GEMIGNANI, R. J. (1973) Perspectives on Delinquency Prevention Strategy. Washington, DC: Government Printing Office.

GOLD, M. (1970) Delinquent Behavior in an American City. Belmont, CA: Brooks/Cole.

HEPBURN, J. R. (1976) "Testing alternative models of delinquency causation." Journal of Criminal Law and Criminology 67: 450-460.

HINDELANG, M. (1973) "Causes of delinquency: a partial replication and extension." Social Problems 20: 471-487.

HIRSCHI, T. (1969) Causes of Delinquency. Berkeley: University of California Press.

HRUSKA, J. (1978) "The obsolescence of adolescence," pp. 65-78 in E. Wenk and N. Harlow (eds.) School Crime and Disruption. Davis, CA: Responsible Action.

KELLY, D. H. (1980) "The educational experience and evolving delinquent careers: a neglected institutional link," pp. 99-114 in D. Shichor and D. Kelly (eds.) Critical Issues in Juvenile Delinquency. Lexington, MA: D. C. Heath.

KORNHAUSER, R. R. (1978) Social Sources of Delinquency. Chicago: University of Chicago Press.

MOOS, R. H. (1975) Evaluating Correctional and Community Settings. New York: John Wiley.

MORASH, M. and S. K. WRIGHT (1982) "The relationships of type of community and labeling to delinquents' participation in community programs: implications for attaining community corrections objectives." Presented at the annual meeting of the American Society of Criminology, Toronto.

MYERS, J. K. and B. H. ROBERTS (1959) Family and Class Dynamics in Mental Illness. New York: John Wiley.

National Advisory Committee on Criminal Justice Standards and Goals (1976) Juvenile Justice and Delinquency Prevention. Washington, DC: Government Printing Office.

PEARL, A., D. GRANT, and E. WENK (1978) The value of Youth. Davis, CA: International Dialogue Press.

SCHWENDINGER, H. and J. SCHWENDINGER (1979) "Delinquency and social reform: a radical perspective," pp. 245-291 in L. T. Empey (ed.) Juvenile Justice: The Progressive Legacy and Current Reforms. Charlottesville: University Press of Virginia.

SEGAL, S. P. and U. AVRIAM (1976) "Community-based sheltered care," pp. 111-124 in P. Ahmed and S. Plog (eds.) State Mental Hospitals. New York: Plenum.

SHAW, C. R. and H. D. McKAY (1931) Social Factors in Juvenile Delinquency. Vol. 2 of Report of the Causes of Crime. National Commission of Law Observance and Enforcement. Washington, DC: Government Printing Office.

SHICHOR, D. (1980) "Some issues of social policy in the field of juvenile delinqueny," pp.317-334 in Critical Issues in Juvenile Delinquency. Lexington, MA: D. C. Heath.

SORRENTINO, A. (1977) Organizing Against Crime: Redeveloping the Neighborhood. New York: Human Sciences Press.

SPERGEL, I. A. (1976) "Interactions between community structure, delinquency and social policy in the inner city," pp. 55-100 in M. Klein (ed.) The Juvenile Justice System. Beverly Hills, CA: Sage.

SPERGEL, I. A. , J. P. LYNCH, F. G. REAMER, and J. KORBELIK (1982) "Response of organization and community to a deinstitutionalization strategy." Crime and Delinquency 28: 426-449.

THRASHER, F. M. (1927) The Gang. Chicago: University of Chicago Press.

WISH, M., M. DEUTSCH, and S. J. KAPLAN (1976) "Perceived dimensions of interpersonal relations." Journal of Personality and Social Psychology 33: 409-420.

Joan McDermott

Seton Hall University

5

THE SERIOUS JUVENILE OFFENDER
Problems in Definition and Targeting

In a prepared statement for the record of the 1978 Senate Hearings on Serious Youth Crime an attorney (Mlyniec, 1978: 98) experienced in the defense of juvenile court clientele wrote:

> Although no one is sure, psychiatrists, social workers and defense lawyers believe, possibly based only on intuition, that the serious violent juvenile offender accounts for only 10 percent of the juvenile court clientele. The first problem is finding him.

If as one part of the social response to crime, something by way of treatment and/or control is to be done with the serious juvenile offender, then indeed the first problem is finding him or her. This is no small problem; it is a task fraught with tensions between intuition and empiricism, public passions and the dictates of justice, budget constraints and system goals, and the all too familiar conflict between treatment and punishment concerns.

"Finding" the serious juvenile offender can be thought of as a two-step process. "Serious juvenile offender" is a construct that first must be conceptually and operationally defined. Second, procedures and processes must be developed for isolating or locating individuals in the population who fit the operational definition. Although this chapter focuses on the first step, the definition of "serious juvenile offender," the definitional process cannot be considered apart from the issues associated with the selection of individuals

AUTHOR'S NOTE: Special thanks to Paul DeMuro of the National Council on Crime and Delinquency for his cooperation and for information on the Violent Juvenile Offenders Project, and to Jeffrey Fagan of the URSA Institute for his critical review of this chapter.

who fit the definitions. This is because serious juvenile offender is a socially created category, a category that exists because various publics—researchers, politicians, citizens, treatment and nontreatment juvenile justice practitioners—have, in different manners, and for somewhat diverse reasons, invented it or targeted it for special consideration. Exactly who are the serious juvenile offenders—how the category is defined and how the individuals are selected—differs considerably depending on who is doing the defining and why, and may ultimately have more to do with practical concerns, political philosophies, and the prevailing winds of public opinion than with empirical research or delinquency theory.

Consider briefly the imprecision in the term "serious juvenile offender." "Serious" itself is a highly ambiguous term which in practice is often used interchangeably with "violent" or "chronic." When used to modify "juvenile offender" or "juvenile crime," the word has been used to mean, among other things, having serious consequences in terms of injury or loss; marked by long duration or frequent recurrence, either of the offense behavior or of the treatment problem; violent; aggressive; dangerous; disruptive or difficult to control in institutions; and resistant or not amenable to treatment. "Serious," when applied to "juvenile offender," derives meaning only through political processes—through the formulating and implementing of laws and official guidelines, and through the selection of certain categories of individuals for special handling in terms of punishment or treatment. Waiver statutes, sentencing prescriptions, program eligibility criteria—these are the mechanisms that give meaning to the term.

"Juvenile" is a less equivocal term, determined largely by court jurisdiction, with the majority of states agreeing that the juvenile status adheres until the eighteenth birthday. However, the term "juvenile" is also a term that is easily manipulable: Statutes define not only who is a juvenile by virtue of age, but also who is excluded from this category either automatically or potentially by virtue of offense behavior and various other criteria found in legislative, judicial, and prosecutorial waiver schemes.

Even the term "offender" is uncertain. Is an arrest sufficient to define a person as an offender? A petition? An adjudication? Criminologists distinguish between official and self-reported offenders.

Examining the problems involved in the definition of the serious juvenile offender can quickly become complex. To introduce some order to this analysis, this chapter is divided into two major sections. The first reviews selected definitions of the serious juvenile offender, focusing on who is doing the defining and why. The second section reviews some of the identification problems and policy issues associated with different definitions. To what extent do different definitions converge to identify specific youths for special handling? How is the construct *serious juvenile offender* transformed into a social reality via programs and policies for treatment and punishment? Here special attention will be given to offender definitions found in the Violent Juvenile Offender Program of the Office of Juvenile Justice and Delinquency Prevention.

DEFINITIONS

There is no universal, widely held, or consistently used definition of "serious juvenile offender," in part because of the diverse perspectives and purposes of the definers. Researchers are concerned primarily with measuring the extent, nature, and trends in serious juvenile crime and the volume and career patterns of serious juvenile offenders. Treatment professionals, coming from a perspective in which serious juvenile offending is a symptom of individual pathology, are concerned with identifying and treating the most diseased patients. Waiver statutes, which in theory represent community moral standards and perceptions of seriousness, and which are generally drafted with a combination of eligibility criteria such as age, offense, and prior record, may also contain reference to treatment (i.e., whether the individual is amenable to treatment within the juvenile justice system). Transfer decisions presumably identify juvenile offenders who, from the standpoint of the community, are so serious (bad, threatening) that they no longer even merit consideration as juveniles. Additional perspectives and definitions of the serious juvenile offender have been offered by a variety of system-related practitioners who come into direct contact with juvenile offenders—police officers, probation officers at intake, defense attorneys, prosecutors, judges, program administrators, institutional staff, and so forth. This section is not intended as a comprehensive review or cataloguing of these definitions and perspectives; rather, it will selectively review some definitions contained in the broad perspectives outlined above.

The Research Perspective

The literature produced by the research community is an important starting point because in recent years there have been a number of efforts to grapple with the problem of defining "serious juvenile offender."[1] A review of this literature quickly reveals the one issue that has most complicated attempts to define the term operationally. Almost always, the serious juvenile offender is defined not as simply as "a juvenile offender who has committed (or is alleged to have committed) a serious offense." If that were the case, only "serious offense" would require specification. However, most definitions also make some degree of repeat offending a defining characteristic of this offender. This produces two conceptually distinct questions:

(1) What is a serious offense?
(2) Who is the serious juvenile offender?

What is a serious offense? Juvenile (under 18)[2] offenses can be thought of as forming a continuum from status offenses to less serious offenses to more serious delinquencies. Because status offenses are automatically excluded from consideration in a definition of serious offense,[3] the problem becomes distinguishing the less serious from the more serious delinquent offenses or crimes.[4]

Operational definitions of a serious offense must link the concept to specific, measurable indicators of severity. It is instructive to consider Zimring's discussion on this point in the proceedings of the 1977 National Symposium on the Serious Juvenile Offender. Zimring evaluated three possible approaches to the definition of serious offenses. The first, involving "the degree to which the individuals involved feel a sense of loss as a result of the infliction of criminal harms," he explains is unacceptable, not only because it is necessarily subjective but also because it is "incapable of being quantified into a scale that can mesh the victim's sense of the severity of crime with the statistics on the incidence of crime and arrest in any aggregate measure" (1977: 16).

The second approach to defining serious offense that is considered by Zimring is the use of a scale to measure the seriousness of individual crime incidents. The scale developed by Sellin and Wolfgang (1964), probably the best known and most widely used of such scales, measures the seriousness of crime incidents through a complex scheme that takes into account such elements as the number of victims of bodily harm and the degree of injury, weapon use, and the dollar value of property stolen, damaged, or destroyed. Scoring the seriousness of incidents of crime this way overcomes some of the difficulties (discussed below) of relying on broad crime categories. Although the Sellin-Wolfgang approach has been taken in some instances,[5] Zimring (1977: 17) is critical of this approach for its inability to provide "lines between serious and nonserious acts" and " a precise cultural consensus on what constitutes serious crime." Although it is true that a point on the seriousness scale would have to be drawn to separate the serious from the nonserious, the first criticism is somewhat unfair: This line will always have to be drawn, and it will always be arbitrary to a degree. His second criticism of seriousness scales, the lack of cultural consensus, may also be unfair given the methodology used to derive the scales. It should be noted that from a measurement perspective, the inadequacies of existing crime data sources and the complexity of the Sellin-Wolfgang scale make it difficult, in practice, to use the scale (Blumstein, 1974).[6]

In defining a serious offense Zimring (1977: 17) chooses a third "value informed" approach; that is, he relies on his own judgement about the severity of offenses and focuses on "the particular forms of adolescent criminal activity that involve serious threats to life or a sense of physical security of victims and potential victims of violent crime." It is interesting to note that these are the same types of criminal acts that would be designated as very serious by seriousness scales; that is, Zimring's definition of serious is highly compatible with, for example, the definitions provided by the samples of evaluators in the Sellin-Wolfgang research. The serious offenses he identifies are homicide, rape, aggravated assault, and robbery.

By so operationalizing the definition of a serious offense Zimring identifies offenses for which both official and unofficial data are routinely collected on a national level.[7] However, this definition is subject to criticism on at least two grounds. First, while consensus certainly exists that human life is more valuable than property, and while there is evidence to suggest that much of the public concern with serious juvenile crime stems from the fear and outrage associated with violent street crime, the definition of "serious" as "violent" is problematic. It is subject not only to the criticism that there is genuine public concern with certain property crimes (e.g., residential burglary, arson) but to the more fundamental criticism that serious simply means more than violent, that perhaps violent offenses are only a subset—a quantitatively small subset—of serious offenses. Smith et al. (1980) review a number of seriousness scales and conclude that the scales agree in suggesting that both violence and property loss be used in defining what is a serious offense. The second major problem with Zimring's definition—one that continues to plague researchers—is that the use of broad offense categories potentially includes many nonserious events. Robberies, for example, vary considerably in terms of injury and loss.

Homicide, rape, aggravated assault, and robbery—Zimring's serious offenses—constitute the Violent Crime Index in the FBI's *Uniform Crime Reports* (UCR). These four violent offenses, together with the Property Index Offenses (burglary, larceny, motor vehicle theft, and arson), make up the UCR Crime Index. The eight index crimes, chosen by the FBI because of their gravity, frequency, and likelihood of being reported to the police, can be thought of as the official or government definition of serious crime in the United States.[8] An example of the use of this UCR or official definition is found in a prepared statement for the 1981 Senate Hearings on Violent Juvenile Crime by Charles A. Lauer, Acting Director of OJJDP: Serious juvenile crime includes the total index offenses, violent juvenile crime includes the violent index offenses, and serious property crime includes the property index offenses (Lauer, 1981: 48).

While the UCR or official definition of serious offenses uses both injury and property loss as definitional criteria, the definition does not differentiate between serious and nonserious offenses within the same offense category.

Moreover, Smith et al. (1980: 27), in an American Justice Institute (AJI) report on serious juvenile crime for the Assessment Center Program of OJJDP, conclude from a careful analysis of the research evidence that

the UCR list of index crimes provides a rough measure of seriousness—except that some crimes *not* on the list may be equally as serious as ones that are on the list. One may also conclude that the three property crimes (burglary, larceny, and auto theft) are in no way as serious as the four violent crimes (homicide, rape, robbery, aggravated assault). . . . It may also be concluded that the Sellin-Wolfgang scale provides a useful measure of degree of seriousness within offense categories as well as a method of scoring individual crime events with their various components of personal injury and property loss.

Smith et al. (1980) attempt to resolve the problem of within-category variation in their definition of serious juvenile offense. The AJI definition excludes certain UCR index crimes—both violent (e.g., unarmed robbery) and property (e.g., petty theft)—that may not merit the label "serious"; it also adds to the list of serious crimes given by the UCR. The report recommends the following definition of serious juvenile offense (1980: 30):

A serious juvenile *offense* includes the following offenses (or ones of at least equal severity) as measured by the Sellin-Wolfgang seriousness scale:

— homicide or voluntary manslaughter
— forcible sexual intercourse
— aggravated assault
— armed robbery
— burglary of an occupied residence
— larceny/theft of more than $1,000
— auto theft without recovery of the vehicle
— arson of an occupied building
— kidnapping
— extortion
— illegal sale of dangerous drugs

The AJI report uses two major criteria for determining what is a serious juvenile offense: violence and property loss. It is not clear how the final offense—illegal sale of dangerous drugs—came to be included in the AJI definition. In the case of a particular offense, the authors recommend that the Sellin-Wolfgang scale be used to determine seriousness, although they do not recommend a particular cutoff point. By excluding many crimes that do not involve significant injury or loss, the AJI definition is a marked improvement over definitions that rely on broad offense categories. Although conceptually neat, the difficulty with the AJI definition, as the authors themselves acknowledge, is that the best available data for describing the nature and extent of juvenile crime use broad UCR categories. It is not possible, for example, to extract from URC arrest data the proportion of larceny thefts involving a loss of more than $1,000. Thus, although the AJI definition or a similar approach to the operationalization of serious offense may in theory be the preferable approach, problems of implementation will necessarily restrict its use.

Who is the serious juvenile offender? The Philadelphia birth cohort research of Woflgang, Figlio, and Sellin published in 1972 drew attention to repeat juvenile offenders. Shown to be responsible for a disproportionately large share of delinquent acts in their communities, repeat offenders became the focus of both research and juvenile justice policy.

Definitions of serious juvenile offender almost always include, in addition to the serious offense criterion, repeat offending. The criterion of repeat behavior is often chronicity, defined as five or more offenses[9] (see Hamparian et al., 1978; Wolfgang et al., 1972; Strasburg, 1978). On the basis of offense history, three offender types can be identified: one-time offenders, repeat offenders (two to four times), and chronic offenders (five or more times).

The task, then, becomes combining the two criteria—offense severity and offense history—in a meaningful way in order to identify the serious juvenile offender. For the moment, assume an acceptable definition of the term serious offense (such as the AJI definition) so that the offense severity variable can be grossly dichotomized into serious and nonserious offenses. Figure 5.1 shows what happens when both offense severity and offense history are considered. Each bar in the figure can be considered an offender type; the length of the bar represents the offender's official record[10] and the shaded area represents the number of officially recorded offenses that are serious offenses. The left-to-right dimension is not a time dimension and is not meant to suggest that serious offenses occur early in a delinquent career. There is no uniform patern of when serious offenses occur in delinquent careers.[11]

Which of the offender types merit the label "serious juveniles offender"? As indicated by the shading in Figure 5.l, the most obvious case is in the bottom righthand corner, the chronic offender with five or more serious offenses on her or his record. But while these offenders no doubt merit the label "serious" according to the criteria above, they exist in very small numbers. In he Ohio cohort study, of the group of youths who had at least one violent arrest, less than 1% had four or more arrests for violence (Hamparian et al., 1978: 5). Moreover, the figure suggests an offender type with *only* serious recorded offenses. But in reality most chronic offenders have records of both serious and nonserious crimes. In the Philadelphia cohort study, only about one-third of the total offenses committed by chronic offenders were index offenses (Wolfgang et al., 1972: 103), and not all index offenses can be considered serious offenses when the actual injury and the loss involved are considered.

So, which of the mixed-record chronic offenders are serious offenders? All of them? Only some of them? Similarly, which of the repeat offenders (two to four times) in Figure 5.1 are serious offenders? In terms of harm, the records of some of them are very similar to the records of some chronic offenders.

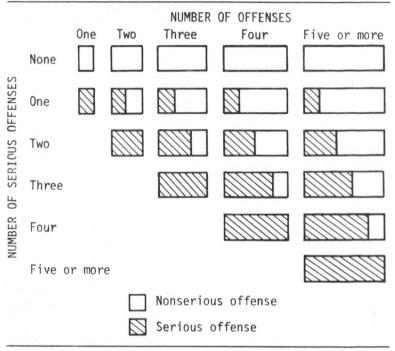

Figure 5.1   Offense History: Number and Seriousness of Recorded Offenses

The chronic nonserious offender in the top righthand corner raises other questions. Should the chronic petty offender be defined as serious because his or her effect on society is cumulatively large? Or should this offender be excluded because she or he has never done anything really "serious"?

The one-time serious offender (first column, second row) is also problematic in terms of defining "serious juvenile offender." Smith et al. (1980: 27) raise the question, "If chronicity or recidivism is made a necessary element of the definition of serious offender, is the first-time offender who commits a murder *not* a serious offender?"

Clearly the use of the two defining criteria—offense severity and offense history— raises a number of questions for which there are no simple answers. In order to resolve some of these problems, in practice the definition of a serious juvenile offender takes on an "either/or" quality in which some measure of the total seriousness of the offense history is taken.

For example, the AJI recommends:[12]

A serious juvenile *offender* is one whose offense history includes adjudication for five or more serious offenses (on the Sellin-Wolfgang scale), or one who is adjudicated for one or more offenses whose severity is equal to homicide or forcible sexual intercourse as measured by the Sellin-Wolfgang scale [Smith et al., 1980: 30].

The use of the Sellin-Wolfgang scale resolves the difficulty of determining which offenders (as suggested in Figure 5.1) are included in the definition of a serious juvenile offender: The cumulative seriousness of the record is the determining factor.

In sum, the serious juvenile offender is viewed as one who has at least one recorded offense that involved the infliction of substantial harm, or one who has an official record containing offenses that cumulatively involve the infliction of substantial harm. The AJI definition does identify those youths whose officially recorded offense behavior has caused the greatest harm, in terms of violence and property loss in the community. The approach excludes those juvenile offenders that simple logic would suggest are not extreme threats to their communities—those with the shortest and least serious offense histories and those with relatively long but cumulatively nonserious offense histories.

It should be noted that because of limitations of existing crime data, there is no way to measure the number or characteristics of serious juvenile offenders in the nation using such a definition, except on a jurisdiction-to-jurisdiction or local level with costly cohort record analysis. Despite the problems of external validity, such research is important in terms of understanding the volume, patterns, and correlates of serious criminal behavior among youths.

Researchers are concerned with counting, classifying, and studying the serious juvenile offender; their definitional problems stem from wanting valid and reliable measurements. Although the research community to a large extent can be said to operate with "eyes down and palms up" (Nicholaus, 1970: 275) and with government agendas and priorities influencing its investigations, the value-free shroud of science grants researchers some immunity from the political pressures that influence other groups who define serious juvenile offender—for example, state legislatures.

The Legislative Perspective

On the state level, the term "serious juvenile offender" is given meaning through two major types of laws: (1) laws that define those youths who are automatically or potentially eligible for adjudication in criminal courts, and (2) laws that define subclassifications of juvenile offenders for special handling (harsher sentences) within the juvenile justice system. The chief difference between the two types of law—whether or not the youth is retained in the juvenile justice system—is a highly significant one. Waiver or transfer statutes answer the question, "When are juveniles not juveniles?" (Zimring, 1981: 193). On some level this involves a determination that the tender loving care and rehabilitative efforts of the juvenile justice system either will not work or will not be enough, that the offender has gone beyond the community's level of tolerance for youthful misconduct, and must be treated (punished) like the criminal she or he is. On the other hand, the creation of special categories of juvenile offenders within the juvenile justice system, with the provision of mandatory penalties, is an attempt to bring together the loving care and rehabilitation of the juvenile justice system with the punishment, incapacitation, and control of the adult system. What the two types of law have in common is essentially a crime control perspective, a perspective that leans heavily on the law—changing laws, adding new laws—to change behavior.

Juvenile court jurisdiction, defined by age, in a handful of states is defined by age and offense; youths who commit certain serious offenses—usually homicide and other capital or life term offenses—are automatically excluded from the definition of "juvenile" (See Biele et al., 1977; Hall et al., 1981). This legislative or automatic waiver gives meaning to the term "serious juvenile offender" by mandating that beyond a certain minimum age, a child is no longer a child if he or she engages in specified serious offenses. Sometimes, as with New York's 1980 Juvenile Offender Law, through a process of reverse waiver, a so-labeled adult-offender youth may be magically transformed back into a juvenile offender, if the criminal court judge finds the case more suitable for disposition in a juvenile court (Roysher and Edelman, 1981).

In most states, waiver or transfer is a judicial decision, made following a hearing on the matter by a juvenile court judge. Here the definition of a serious juvenile offender is determined largely on a case-by-case basis, and unlike legislative waiver, much more than statutorily defined seriousness is taken into consideration.[13] A comparative analysis of juvenile codes by the Community Research Forum (1980: 12) found that the most common waiver criteria include

> (1) lack of rehabilitation or suitable facilities or services for the juvenile charged; (2) the ability of the juvenile justice system to rehabilitate the child; (3) the best interests of the child and the public; (4) the seriousness of the offense; (5) protection of the public; (6) whether the juvenile probably committed the offense; (7) the juvenile's record and history (and probable cause of behavior), his or her physical and mental maturity, demeanor, and age; and (8) whether the juvenile is commitable to an institution or is retarded or insane.

The statutory criteria that guide judicial transfer decisions are generally broad; however, the factors that seem to be most important are the seriousness of the offense and the youth's prior record (Davis, 1981: 251), the same factors suggested by the research definitions above. Nevertheless, it is possible under most waiver provisions that a youth technically eligible for waiver may find that transfer hinges on factors beyond her or his control, specifically the availability of facilities or services in the juvenile and adult systems (Davis, 1981; Rubin, 1979). For example, the Institute of Judicial Administration and American Bar Association (IJA-ABA) Juvenile Justice Standards suggest the following waiver criteria (in Davis, 1981: 251):

1. the seriousness of the alleged class one juvenile offense;

2. a prior record of adjudicated delinquency involving the infliction or threat of significant bodily injury;

3. the likely inefficacy of dispositions available to the juvenile court as demonstrated by previous dispositions of the juvenile; and

4. the appropriateness of the services and dispositional alternatives available in the criminal justice system for dealing with the juvenile's problems, and whether they are, in fact available.

So reasons for waiver may go beyond considerations of offense severity and priors, to include vestiges of the medical model (treatment needs, amenability to treatment) and organizational resource concerns (available services and facilities).

When legislatures in recent years have responded to the problem of serious delinquency by creating special categories of "violent" or "repeat" offenders for harsher sentences, almost always some combinations of age, offense severity, and prior record are definitional criteria (see examples in Rubin, 1979: 25-26.) However, resource considerations are also involved. A report of the Minnesota Governor's Commission on Crime Prevention and Crime Control (Biele et al., 1977) highlights implications of different definitions of "violent" or "hard-core" juvenile offenders. One of the criteria used for evaluating various definitions was the following:

Does the definition result in a number of juveniles which is small enough in proportion to the total juvenile offender population to make differential treatment a feasible alternative? [1977: 18].

"Numbers"—small enough, or , as we will see in another context, big enough—is a type of practical concern frequently employed in the rationalization of juvenile justice policy. What "small enough" means in terms of the proportion of total juvenile offenders who are labeled serious varies dramatically from one jurisdiction to another on the basis of such factors as total number of juvenile offenders in the population and the resources available for alternative treatment programs.

The definition of violent or hard-core offender recommended by the Minnesota group (Biele et al., 1977: 18) includes juveniles 14 and over who

— have a sustained petition involving one of the following four offenses: homicide, kidnapping, aggravated arson, or criminal sexual conduct in the first or third degree.
— or who have a sustained petition for manslaughter, aggravated assault or aggravated robbery, with a prior record within the past twenty-four months of a sustained felony.
— or who have had at least two separate adjudications involving at least three major property offenses.

The types of crime included in this definition were chosen on the basis of their severity (quanified in terms of maximum sentences given by the penal law). A comparison of the definition of the Minnesota group with the AJI definition of a serious juvenile offender reveals a number of differences, the most striking of which appear to be the methods by which offense severity and repetitiveness are operationalized and combined as criteria in either/or formats. Statutorily defined seriousness (serious quantified in terms of penal sanctions) may differ considerably from research defined seriousness (e.g., seriousness scales).

In addition to differing from research definitions of serious juvenile offender, statutory definitions—whether they be through various waiver mechanisms or through laws providing for harsher treatment within the juvenile justice system—can be expected to vary considerably from one state to another. Dick and Jane may be serious juvenile offenders if they live in New York but not if they live in Connecticut. This is an important consideration because, unlike research definitions that exist for counting purposes, legislative definitions exist for punishment and control purposes and have major consequences in terms of what happens to Dick and Jane.

The Treatment Perspective

While medical model concepts (treatment needs, amenability to treatment) may come into play in legislative definitions, they are the central concepts in definitions of the term "serious juvenile offender" offered from a treatment perspective. In the medical model, crime is a symptom of individual pathology, and "wayward youths who have committed any type of crime should be treated as though they had a disease"(Bartollas and Miller, 1978: 13). Because within the medical model the serious juvenile offender is defined by the treatment problem he or she presents, offense seriousness and offense history may become secondary considerations.

There is no single treatment definition of a serious juvenile offender, in part because the individual pathology is variously described in terms of biological, psychological, and sociocultural factors, alone or in combination, and because treatment may go beyond the individual to his or her interactions with significant others (e.g., family, friends) and environment (neighborhood). There is no single factor "cause" and no one "cure" (Goins, 1977). Because there is no central or best definition from a treatment perspective, some examples will serve to illustrate this approach.

In line with the movement toward deinstitutionalization and community treatment, a number of studies have concluded that from the standpoint of public safety, only a small minority of youths require secure confinement (Strasburg, 1978; Missouri Law Enforcement Assistance Council, 1971; Ohlin et al., 1977; Abt Associates, 1976). It is perhaps no surprise that this small minority is also the group identified by treatment professionals as youths sorely in need of the kind of treatment available only in secure confinement. From a treatment perspective (Vachss and Bakal, 1979: 39), "when operationally defined, societal needs and those of delinquent children may well converge in certain cases to indicate incarceration in a secure treatment facility." One approach to the definition of a serious juvenile offender from a treatment framework is to look at descriptions of delinquent youth who (coincidentally) for their own best interests as well as the community's "need" confinement.

Manella (1977: 14-15) describes the "hard-core" or "hyperaggressive" juveniles "who require care in a physically restricting facility" in terms of a mental health profile "based upon empirical data and observations accumulated over the years in studies of state juvenile correctional institutions." In general terms, the profile describes hard-core, hyperaggressive delinquents as adolescents who

1. Are burdened with special additional problems as they grow and develop to full maturity.

2. Have long histories of delinquent, criminal, and deviant behavior.

3. Have acquired deeply-rooted anti-social values and attitudes.

4. Are agitated personalities with character defects and are unwilling or unable to control themselves in group settings.

5. Are hostile, alienated personalities.

6. Are habitual law violators, runaways, and from families well known to police, mental health, welfare, and court-correctional officials.

7. Are sometimes superficially passive and suave, concealing but not visibly acting out their hostility [1977: 15-16].

Unlike the research definitions that include both violent and property offenders in the term "serious," the treatment perspective tends to focus on offenders who are considered violent or dangerous. Vachss and Bakal (1979) are concerned with chronic, violent offenders who require specialized treatment in a Secure Treatment Unit. Based on their experiences working with youth in Massachusetts, they describe the "life-style violent juvenile" as one who is "characterized by a distortion of societal values, a commitment to immediate gratification, and a (reinforced) alienation from societal structures and institutions" (1979: 15). Additionally, Vachss and Bakal (1979: 34) suggest that the term "rehabilitation" is inappropriate in treatment of the life-style violent juvenile, because the term suggests restoration or reestablishment:

> The life-style violent juvenile lives a feral, atavistic, existence. He is responsive only to immediate situations and not to any larger societal pressures. Very often he is hostile, fearful, and (as a result) dangerous. . . . But our goal is not to return him to former behavior, but to give him the means, motive, and opportunity to participate in the *changing* of such behavior.

The "hard-core, hyperaggressive" (Manella, 1977) and the "life-style violent" (Vachss and Bakal, 1979) juvenile offenders are both described in terms of exhibiting hostility, aggression, and dangerousness; both are violence-prone, alienated, and have deep-seated problems; both are disruptive and difficult to control. Elsewhere, aggressive and violent youth have been described as the most difficult youths from a correctional worker's perspective (Ho, 1975; McCleary, 1975; Tennenbaum, 1978). It would appear, then, that in terms of treatment these are the serious juvenile offenders.

This raises some interesting questions. If from a treatment point of view serious means violent, hostile, dangerous, and/or aggressive, where does the serious property offender (e.g., the six-time residential burglar) fit in? On the one hand, the logic of this perspective suggests that the recurrent offense behavior is symptomatic of chronic illness, or "serious" pathology. On the other hand, if the youth is not violent or dangerous, does she or he have a serious treatment problem? More fundamentally, if the illness (not the offense) is the central concern in the treatment perspective, what happens definitionally when there is a lack of correspondence between the seriousness of the offense (or the chronicity) and the seriousness of the illness? Is it possible for a one-time property offender, or even a juvenile status offender, to have the same treatment needs as a chronic, violent offender?

In summary, this section has selectively reviewed definitions of serious juvenile offender within three broad perspectives: research, legislative, and treatment. Because researchers define in order to count and classify, legislators define in order to punish and control, and treatment professionals define in order to cure, the three perspectives arrive at somewhat different definitions of a serious juvenile offender. The perspectives, to some extent, do agree that offense seriousness and behavioral history are considerations in identifying the serious juvenile offender, although definitions may differ in terms of what is a serious offense, how exactly behavioral history is of concern, and how central these factors are to the definitions. The perspectives also vary in terms of any additional defining criteria, such as age, available services, considerations of individual pathology, and so forth.

PROBLEMS AND ISSUES IN IDENTIFICATION AND TARGETING

The preceding section introduced three broad perspectives on the definition of the serious juvenile offender. To the extent that these and other perspectives converge to identify the same individuals, and to the extent that justice system policies and procedures work to select out of the population of youths those who fit the definitions, the serious juvenile offender is transfromed from a social construct to a social reality—we "find" the serious juvenile offender. In theory, a number of likely gains flow from successful identification and targeting.

The system would be more efficient; by directing its efforts on the worst cases, the repeat offenders who are responsible for more than their share of harm, the justice system would reap the largest return on its investment of resources. System (juvenile justice system) practitioners would be happy for other reasons. If something could be done with the problem of serious juvenile crime, and especially if that something could be done *within* the juvenile justice system, defenders of the juvenile court would be able to counter claims that the court is outmoded, that it has proven so ineffective that it should be abolished.

There are, of course, potential benefits for the youths identified and handled as serious juvenile criminals, especially as more knowledge accumulates about what to do with them. There may even be payoffs for nonserious offenders. It need not be the case that in dealing more harshly with its serious offenders the system becomes more punitive for all. For example, recent juvenile justice reform in New Jersey, although dealing largely with serious juvenile offenders (making it easier to transfer cases to the criminal court), retained the rehabilitative ideal and mandated significantly improved services for the nonserious offenders.

But a variety of problems and issues arise in identifying serious juvenile offenders and selecting them for special handling, either in terms of treatment or in terms of punishment. Some issues are moral and political, some very practical, some legal. Other problems arise because of the lack of correspondence between the dictates of public policy and the findings of social research. Because of the current emphasis in juvenile justice on dealing with the serious juvenile offender, we can begin to identify some of the problems and issues in definition and targeting by looking at some recent policy reforms and programs.

At the outset, strategies fall into two broad categories: those that deal with serious juvenile offenders by transferring them to the jurisdiction of the adult court, and those that retain them in the juvenile justice system. The problems and issues surrounding the first category—waiver—have been discussed elsewhere in great detail (Hall et al., 1982) and will not be reviewed here. However, it is important at this juncture to make a few general points with respect to waiver. First, in terms of what actually happens to a youth, the decision whether or not to define the offender as an adult may be the most significant decision made by the system, and so should be a reasoned decision made with great care and procedural fairness. However, as a second point, experience with waiver suggests that the difficulties associated with this strategy virtually ensure that the targeted youth are selected through processes that are unreasonable and unfair. Roysher and Edelman (1981: 266), for example, report on some of the consequences of the 1978 Juvenile Offender Law in New York:[14] The law brought more delayed, complex, and less-efficient processing; generated considerable sentencing disparities; and increased the discretion of prosecutors, judges, and administrative agencies. Third, because of the numerous negotiated decisions (e.g., arrest, charging) surrounding the definition, it is probable that those youths with the least power and the fewest resources to bring to negotiations (poor and minority youths) are more likely to be targeted (Hairston, 1981). (Of course, it should be noted that to the degree that all system-identified serious juvenile offenders are targeted through negotiated definitions, similar problems occur whether or not the youth is transferred to the adult court.)

What kind of definitional problems are involved in policy and program reforms and innovations that handle the serious juvenile offender within the juvenile justice system? To lend some substance to this discussion, it is helpful to consider some of the issues that have surfaced in an operating program.

THE VIOLENT JUVENILE OFFENDER PROGRAM

Probably the best and most timely example is the $4 million federally funded Violent Juvenile Offender Program (VJOP). The 1980 Senate amendments to the Juvenile Justice and Delinquency Act directed the Office of Juvenile Justice and Delinquency Prevention (OJJDP) to develop programs aimed at curbing serious crime by juveniles. Through OJJDP, "the juvenile justice system should give additional attention to the problem of juveniles who commit serious crimes, with particular attention given to the areas of sentencing, providing resources necessary for informed dispositions, and rehabilitation" (Public Law 96-509, Section 101 (a) (8)). The act defines serious crime as "criminal homicide, forcible rape, mayhem, kidnapping, aggravated assault, robbery, larceny or theft punishable as a felony, motor vehicle theft, burglary or breaking and entering, extortion accompanied by threats of violence, and arson punishable as a felony" (Section 103 (14)).

OJJDP developed the VJOP in response to this congressional mandate. However, the focus of the VJOP is on chronic, violent offenders, thereby excluding many youths who might be considered serious juvenile offenders (e.g., serious property offenders). While it is not clear exactly how OJJDP came to center its efforts on this offender type, it is likely that the violent focus came from growing public and legislative concern with juvenile violence, and the chronic came from a concern with identifying "truly" violent rather than episodically violent youth.

The part of the VJOP[15] that is designed to test intervention strategies with chronic, violent juvenile offenders is a cooperative effort (the VJO Consortium) of OJJDP, the funding agency, which has responsibility for overall policy; the National Council on Crime and Delinquency (NCCD), which serves as national coordinator and has overall administrative responsibility; the National Organization for Social Responsibility (NOSR), the technical assistance contractor; and URSA Institute, which is responsible for evaluating the program. Beginning in October 1980, the VJO Consortium assessed the existing information on violent juvenile crime, and based on that information defined the target population for the initiative, established the intervention strategy to be tested, and developed application procedures and selection criteria (OJJDP, 1981: 11). As part of a 36-month research and development program, five projects, located in areas with high rates of violent youth crime,[16] were to be selected to receive assistance in program development and operation and were to be systematically monitored and evaluated (OJJDP, 1981: 11). The Request for Proposals (RFP) of OJJDP in April 1981 defined the target population of the VJOP as "chronic, violent juvenile offenders" (1981: 12):

1. *Violent.* Violent offenses are: first and second degree homicide, kidnap, forcible rape or sodomy, aggravated assault (with a weapon and/or resulting in serious bodily harm), armed robbery, and arson of an occupied structure.

2. *Chronic.* For all violent offenses other than first degree murder, chronicity involves an adjudicated violent instant offense and at least one prior adjudication or conviction for a violent offense. For first degree murder, no prior history of violence is required.

3. *Juvenile.* A juvenile is a person who has not yet reached his or her 18th birthday.

4. *Offender.* To be considered an eligible offender, a juvenile must have committed the instant offense prior to age 18 and have been adjudicated delinquent.

Note especially that the RFP definition of chronic involves an adjudicated instant offense of violence and at least *one* prior adjudication or conviction for a violent offense. This differs from research "five or more" concept of chronic. The "five or more" concept is based on arrests, and it was felt that adjudications would be a more useful standard for identifying comparable groups across sites. Also, the definition includes some one-time offenders, those for whom the instant offense is first-degree murder.

Five project sites were selected by the VJO Consortium through a stringent preapplication, application, site visit process: Phoenix, Denver, Boston, Newark, and Memphis. The projects were all operating by the first quarter of 1982. What, then, were the major targeting issues?

"Too Few of the Violent Few!" In a series of meetings prior to the release of the RFP, the VJO Consortium carefully examined its target population definition, debating both important conceptual issues (whether a youth requires a prior record to be deemed violent) and methodological concerns (whether the proposed definition would so restrict the potential population as to make the experimental and control groups too small). Evaluation was to be a key component of the VJOP, and the impact of the definition on the samples sizes at the sites was an especially important concern for URSA, the evaluators, as too small sample sizes would prohibit random assignment to experimental and control groups and would limit the statistical analysis.

These early fears were realized when in early 1982 the programs began operating. By late April, concerns over slow intake at the sites resulted in an expansion of the eligibility criteria. Two offenses (attempted murder and attempted rape) were added to the instant offense list, and the list of eligible priors was broadened to include all nonvehicular manslaughter, felonious assault, robbery, mayhem, and violent sexual abuse. Although this expansion helped Boston and Newark, by late May the Memphis and Phoenix projects were still experiencing intake problems. The Phoenix project was allowed to expand geographically in hopes of improving its sample size. By late May the Denver contract had been cancelled due to the small numbers problem, and the VJO Consortium began considering selecting another site. Finally, by this time a second expansion of eligibility criteria was recommended. Approved by OJJDP early in June, the expansion is in terms of the meaning of "chronicity," which was broadened to include both petitions and the serious property crimes listed in the Juvenile Justice and Delinquency Prevention Act. Thus, the definition was ultimately expanded to include the more widely accepted notion of serious juvenile offender (person and/or property offenses, prior record), while the spirit of the initiative—its emphasis on violent offenders—was retained by maintaining a violent instant offense.

By late September 1982, there had been no additional alterations in eligibility criteria. The expanded definition helped the numbers of experimental cases in Memphis, Boston, Newark and Phoenix. No decision had yet been made regarding a new fifth site, although the VJO Consortium was considering a few.

"Too Few" is both good news and bad news—good news from the standpoint of dispelling popular myths and fears surrounding violent juvenile crime, but bad news for the VJOP. Perhaps the consortium could have chosen larger cities as project sites.[17] Maybe the original target population should not have been as narrowly defined as "chronic, violent," particularly in terms of violent priors.

Even alternative operational definitions of chronicity might have resulted in both adequate case flow and , more important, a more accurate identification of the chronically violent target population. Perhaps. This is the argument presented by J. Michael Whitaker, Project Director of the Shelby County Violent Offender Project (the Memphis project). Whitaker (1982: 2) argues that "the 'letter' by which the population guidelines were constructed at times prohibits full realization of the 'intent' of the guidelines." In other words, Whitaker expresses concern about the VJOP guidelines resulting in a number of false negatives—youths who are actually chronically violent being rejected. Whitaker notes that the primary problem is with the definition of chronic:

> With the focus on prior history, we are left with the task of interacting with the past. Such interaction usually occurs through each youth's court files which may or may not adequately describe the events of the prior offenses. Even in the most complete files, it is still impossible, however, to observe the dynamics of the various interactions which occurred around the prior offenses [1982: 15].

It seems that once the decision is made to keep a youth in juvenile court, precision in charging and recording offenses is no longer an important consideration. Because juvenile court record-keeping is notoriously poor in reflecting what really happened, it should come as no surprise that a target population definition that focuses on "prior record" would miss many youths who were, in fact, chronically violent. (Add to this the number of youths who have histories of *unofficial* violent offenses and the number of false negatives is considerably larger, although by definition unrecorded or undetected delinquency is not prior record, and there is plainly no legal or practically feasible way to include unofficial delinquency in eligibility criteria.)

Whitaker's proposal would expand the VJOP concept of chronicity in two ways. First, it would include *situational* chronicity (1982: 16): "situations in which the violence involved in the instant offense is sufficiently extreme to remove most doubts concerning the extent to which the involved youth has incorporated violence as part of his routine behavior." Second, it would include *proportional* chronicity, a sequence of two or more adjudications for "person" offenses occurring in a minimum four-month period prior to the instant offense.

Whitaker's definitions are offered from the perspective of a project director concerned with developing eligibility criteria that work to include the truly chronically violent. These definitions had to be rejected by the VJO Consortium both because they were thought to have the potential for so expanding the definition of chronicity as to result in many false positives (accepting youths who were not, in actuality, chronically violent) and because of the enormous difficulties in ensuring consistent interpretation of the concepts (especially situational chronicity) across research sites.

The national VJOP is a 36-month research and development program. When the projects have been evaluated and when the history of the VJOP initiative has been written, it will surely illustrate many targeting and definition problems. For now, it is apparent that programs that have as their target population chronic, violent youths will have to face squarely the issues of conceptualization (What do we mean by chronic, by violent?), operationalization (How can we measure chronicity with the information that is available?), and feasibility (given our definitions, do the numbers justify the program?).

Briefly: additional targeting issues. In closing, attempts to develop special programs for serious juvenile offenders raise other targeting or eligibility issues.

1. A major question involves the use of system response definitions versus theoretical definitions (Whitaker, 1982). System response definitions (e.g., in terms of adjudications or petitions) are based on the tenuous assumption that the various decision points or components in the system work as they should—that there are no slip-ups in law enforcement, intake, prosecution, adjudication, and so forth. On the other hand, definitions derived from theories of delinquency are often based on concepts that are difficult to measure reliably (e.g., needs, traits, strains, deficiencies). It is an open question whether it is easier to change the system so that it functions properly or to develop instrumentation for the theoretical definitions.

2. If it is likely that the targeting will result in harsher treatment within the juvenile justice system, it is also likely that *processing* will be more complex, involving more frequent delays. For example, juveniles facing secure commitment would be more likely to deny the allegations in the petition (Biele et al., 1977). Plea bargaining might also increase, further complicating accurate indentification of juveniles who commit serious crimes.

3. Other concerns are related to "treatment" versus "punishment." In the current punishing social climate, it becomes increasingly difficult to justify retaining offenders in the juvenile justice system; but transfer raises another whole set of targeting issues, as suggested above. When is a child not a child? On the other hand, if treatment alternatives for serious juvenile offenders are developed within the juvenile justice system, especially alternatives with some period of secure confinement (the public safety concern), how can states justify waiver to criminal court (Biele et al., 1977)?

4. Numerous resource concerns are involved. Cost is a big issue. Are new secure facilities for juveniles justified in light of projected declines or stabilization in serious juvenile offending? Would scarce public monies be better spent on system change research and development programs or on testing alternative treatment strategies? In the end, do the numbers of serious juvenile offenders justify any major change in policy or expenditure of funds?

5. Moral and political issues derive from the inevitable associations among poverty, race-ethnicity, and definitions of seriousness. To the extent that program-policy targeting involves negotiation (and in the end it always does), social, political, and economic power are important variables in terms of who is defined as a serious juvenile offender. Yet with few exceptions, the implications of this have rarely been addressed in the literature on serious juvenile offenders.

NOTES

1. The following discussion draws heavily on an unpublished report by McDermott and Joppich (1980).

2. To simplify the discussion, the "under 18" cutoff point for juvenile court jurisdiction and definition of "juvenile" will be used in this chapter.

3. Note, however, that especially in some treatment-oriented definitions, the notion of chronicity may be dangerously close to the notion of "incorrigibility."

4. Although nonstatus juvenile offenses are "delinquencies," not "crimes," the word crime will be used here for purposes of clarity.

5. The definition suggested by Smith et al., (1980) relies in part on the Sellin-Wolfgang scale. This will be discussed later.

6. Although the potential for such analysis exists with the National Crime Survey victimization data, this data set has its own limitations, particularly if the objective is to arrive at counts of offenders.

7. Uniform Crime Report and National Crime Survey data are the official and unofficial data sources that routinely collect information on these offenses.

8. Arguably, there are other crimes—for example, certain corporate crimes, that may be said to be more serious in terms of loss and injury—however, the FBI's Crime Index is undeniably the official government definition of serious crime in the United States.

9. Hamparian et al., (1978: 5) define a chronic offender as one with five or more offenses; Strasberg (1978: 9) defines a chronic delinquent as one with "five or more charges in his record"; and Wolfgang et al., (1972: 88) counted as chronic recidivists "those with 5 officially recorded delinquencies or more."

10. Of course, many offenses go undetected and unrecorded; this will be discussed later.

11. Usually this is discussed in terms of escalation or progression from less to more serious offending. However, available evidence suggests that delinquents do not progress uniformly from bad to worse.

12. Note that this definition uses "adjudications" and not arrests. The difficulties of relying on juvenile court files to identify serious juvenile offenders will be discussed later.

13. It should be noted that under systems of legislative or automatic waiver, the prosecutor's charging decision (what to charge) is extremely important, and because of this legislative definitions are not as clear-cut as they appear.

14. The law mandated original adult court jurisdiction for juveniles of certain ages (as low as 13 for murder or 15 for other violent offenses) charged with designated violent felonies.

15. Part I of the VJOP is designed to test intervention strategies with chronic violent offenders. Part II deals with prevention of violent juvenile crime and is administered separately. It is Part I that is the subject of the subsequent discussion.

16. The 1981 RFP of OJJDP was sent to state and local correctional agencies with jurisdiction over chronic, violent juvenile offenders in 49 cities with 3,000 or more reported violent index crimes according to UCR data (OJJDP, 1981: 3).

17. Sites were selected competitively. New York, Chicago, Washington, and Los Angeles all bid unsuccessfully. Detroit, Philadelphia, Houston, and other eligible cities did not apply.

REFERENCES

Abt Associates (1976) The Camp Hill Project: An Assessment. Washington, DC: U.S. Law Enforcement Assistance Administration.

BARTOLLAS, C. and S. J. MILLER (1978) The Juvenile Offender: Control, Correction, and Treatment. Boston: Allyn & Bacon.

BIELE, L. C. et al. (1977) Alternative Definitions of "Violent" or "Hard-core" Juvenile Offenders: Some Empirical and Legal Implications. Research report by the Juvenile Justice Research Team, Minnesota Governor's Commission on Crime Prevention and Control, St. Paul, MN.

BLUMSTEIN, A. (1974) "Seriousness weights in an index of crime." American Sociological Review 39: 854-864.

Community Research Forum (1980) A Comparative Analysis of Juvenile Codes. Washington DC: Government Printing Office.

DAVIS, S. M. (1981) "Legal and procedural issues related to the waiver process,"pp. 227-264 in J. C. Hall et al. (eds.) Major Issues in Juvenile Justice Information and Training: Readings in Public Policy. Columbus, OH: Academy For Contemporary Problems.

GOINS, S. (1977) "The serious or violent juvenile offender—is there a treatment response?" pp. 130-147 in The Serious Juvenile Offender, Proceedings of a National Symposium held in Minneapolis, Minnesota on September 19 and 20. U.S. Law Enforcement Assistance Administration.

HAIRSTON, G. E. (1981) "Black crime and the New York State Juvenile Offender Law: a consideration of the effects of lowering the age of criminal responsibility," pp. 227-264 in J. C. Hall et al. (eds.) Major Issues in Juvenile Justice Information and Training: Readings in Public Policy. Columbus, OH: Academy For Contemporary Problems.

HALL, J. C. et al. [eds.] (1981) Major Issues in Juvenile Justice Information and Training: Readings in Public Policy. Columbus OH: Academy for Contemporary Problems.

HAMPARIAN, D. M. et al. (1978) The Violent Few: A Study of Dangerous Juvenile Offenders. Lexington, MA: D. C. Heath.

HO, M. K. (1975) "Aggressive behavior and violence of youth: aproaches and alternatives." Federal Probation 39, 1: 24-28.

LAUER, C. A. (1981) Prepared Statement on Violent Juvenile Crime Hearing before the Subcommittee on Juvenile Justice, July 9. Washington DC: Government Printing Office.

McCLEARY, R. D. (1975) "Violent youth." International Journal of Offender Therapy and Comparative Criminology 19, 1: 81-86.

McDERMOTT, M. J. and G. JOPPICH (1980) The serious Juvenile Offender. Hackensack, N.J.: National Council on Crime and Delinquency.

MANELLA, R. L. (1977) The Hard-Core Juvenile Offender. Reno, NV: National Council of Juvenile Court Judges.

Missouri Law Enforcement Assistance Council (1971) Proposed High Security Training Schools for Youth in Trouble. Jefferson City, MO: Task Force on Juvenile Delinquency.

MLYNIEC, W. J. (1978) Prepared statement for the Serious Youth Crime Hearings before the Subcommittee to Investigate Juvenile Delinquency, April 10 and 12. Washington DC: Government Printing Office.

NICHOLAUS, M. (1970) "Text of a speech delivered a the A.S.A. Convention, August 26, 1968," pp. 274-278 in L. T. Reynolds and J. M. Reynolds (eds.) The Sociology of Sociology. New York: David McKay.

OHLIN, L. E., A. D. MILLER and R. B. COATES (1977) Juvenile Correctional Reform in Massachusetts. Washington, DC: U.S. Office of Juvenile Justice and Delinquency Prevention.

ROYSHER, M. P. EDELMAN (1981) "Treating juveniles as adults in New York: what does it mean and how does it work?" pp. 265-293 in J. C. Hall et al. (eds.) Major Issues in Juvenile Justice Information and Training: Readings in Public Policy. Columbus OH: Academy for Contemporary Problems.

RUBIN, H. T. (1979) Juvenile Justice: Policy Practice and Law. Santa Monica, CA: Goodyear.

SELLIN, T. and M. E. WOLFGANG (1964) The Measurement of Delinquency. New York: John Wiley.

SMITH, C. P. et al. (1980) A National Assessment of Serious Juvenile Crime and the Juvenile Justice System: The Need for a Rational Response (Vol. II: Definition, Characteristics of Incidents and Individuals and Relationship to Substance Abuse). Washington, DC: U. S. Office of Juvenile Justice and Delinquency Prevention.

STRASBURG, P. A. (1978) Violent Delinquents. New York: Monarch.

TENNENBAUM, D. J. (1978) " 'Dangerousness' within a juvenile institution." Journal of Criminal Justice 6, 4: 329-345.

U.S. Office of Juvenile Justice and Delinquency Prevention (1981) Violent Juvenile Offender Program (Part 1): Request for Proposals. Washington, DC: U.S. Department of Justice, Office of Juvenile Justice and Delinquency Prevention.

VACHSS, A. H. and Y. BAKAL (1979) The Life-Style Violent Juvenile. Lexington, MA: D. C. Heath.

WHITAKER, J. M. (1982) "Position paper: an overview of the definition of chronic violent offender following seventeen weeks of screening in Shelby County, Tennessee." Shelby County Violent Offender Project, Memphis, TN.

WOLFGANG, M. E., R. M. FIGLIO, and T. SELLIN (1972) Delinquency in a Birth Cohort. Chicago: University of Chicago Press.

ZIMRING, F. E. (1981) "Notes toward a jurisprudence of waiver" pp. 193-206 in J. C. Hall, et al. (eds.) Major Issues in Juvenile Justice Information and Training: Readings in Public Policy. Columbus, OH: Academy for Contemporary Problems.

——— (1977) "The serious juvenile offender: notes on an unknown quantity," pp. 15-31 in The Serious Juvenile Offender, Proceedings of a National Symposium held in Minneapolis, Minnesota, on September 19 and 20. U. S. Law Enforcement Assistance Administration.

6

Jeffrey Fagan

Karen V. Hansen

Michael Jang

URSA Institute

PROFILES OF CHRONICALLY VIOLENT JUVENILE OFFENDERS
An Empirical Test of an Integrated Theory of Violent Delinquency

Violent juvenile offenders have recently become the center of juvenile justice system attention and legislative action. While concern about youth crime has historically been great, the intense public reaction in the late 1970s has generated a major shift in the basic premises of the juvenile justice system (Sublett, 1977). The shift is away from the concept of *parents patriae* and rehabilitative ideals of the juvenile court to the punitive-retributive philosophy of the adult court. Accompanying this shift is increasing utilization of the bellweather of the entire correctional system—secure confinement (Vachss and Bakal, 1979; Miller and Ohlin, 1980). In many states, new laws have been passed mandating either longer periods of more secure confinement for juveniles adjudicated delinquent for violent offenses, or easing their transfer requirements to adult court jurisdiction (Hamparian, 1982). From this emerging emphasis on harsher punishment for violent juveniles, we can conclude that the juvenile justice system has replaced the long-honored concepts of "aid, encouragement and guidance" with greater emphasis on considerations of personal safety and community protection.

AUTHORS' NOTE: This research was supported by Grant #80-JN-AX-0006 from the National Institute for Juvenile Justice and Delinquency Prevention, Office of Juvenile Justice and Delinquency Prevention, U. S. Department of Justice. The opinions and views are those of the authors and do not reflect the position of the Department of Justice. We wish to thank the field researchers who collected the data analyzed here: Susan Guarino, Gregg Halemba, Karen Rich and Linda Sheridan.

Despite the fact that violent juvenile offenders constitute a relatively small and identifiable group, juvenile courts and corrections agencies have largely neglected to differentiate these youth and provide unique dispositions and services. Given limited resources and high caseloads, the juvenile justice system has handled these youth much like other, nonviolent offenders, often with little or no effect (e.g., Robison and Smith, 1971; Lerman, 1975). These practices are based largely on theories of delinquency causation and rehabilitative models that assume that all delinquent behaviors—violent and nonviolent, "status" offenses, or criminal acts—share common causal factors and etiological roots. It could well be, however, that such undifferentiated theories and practices may be responsible for the well-documented failure of treatment programs for violent delinquents (Gottfredson, 1979). Numerous evaluations of evaluations have cited weak methodology, inappropriate or insensitive measures, and poor analytic approaches as causes for skepticism about claims of treatment effectiveness or prospects for identifying and reintegrating violent delinquents (Sechrest and Redner, 1978). However, while assessment of treatment effectiveness has historically proven elusive, a recurring theme in these critiques is that such failures result more often from a "poverty of theory than a dearth of methodological skill" (Glaser, 1973).

The failure of the juvenile courts and correctional agencies to respond effectively to violent youths can be traced to the absence of empirical knowledge and viable theory of the causes of violent delinquency. This in turn underlies the failure of treatment. The development of such knowledge could dramatically impact delinquency policy. For example, it could validate a method to identify, control, and reintegrate the most dangerous juvenile offenders. The purpose of this chapter is to synthesize earlier work on violent delinquency, build on the precepts of an integrated theory, and begin the process of empirical specification and elaboration.

Theories of Delinquency
and Theories of Violence

A fundamental pursuit in criminology and the study of delinquency is the pursuit of causes (Haskell and Yablonsky, 1978). Since 1899, youths who violated the law were placed under the relatively benign wing of the juvenile court. There, the disapproved behavior was treated as a family or community problem, regardless of why the act occurred or whether it involved a violation of parental authority or a violent crime. The theories that guided the traditional juvenile court response were based on vague perceptions of all juvenile delinquents as products of various sets of causes, all of which are presumed to affect a broad range of youths equally and which lead to a predictable range of behaviors. Treatment responses to delinquent youths also reflected this unicausal view of widely varying behaviors.

Today, despite the growth of a complex social system to deal with juvenile delinquency, an omnibus delinquency theory still prevails. Responses to delinquent youth are based on a uniform set of presumed causes irrespective of offense type. Only recently has delinquency policy attempted to link sanction with the behavior rather than individual offender profiles. Yet this policy shift does not resolve some basic questions about the causes and cures of either violence or delinquency. Implicit in the recent national spate of legislation to deal specifically with violent juveniles is the belief that they somehow differ from other delinquents and require harsher (and more secure) confinement. Moreover, it suggests that the prevention or treatment of violent juvenile crime should rely on different theories and strategies designed exclusively for this population. Yet their theoretical precepts are unclear, and there is little empirical support for such assertions and practices. Are violent juveniles different from juvenile delinquents? Our task in this chapter is to ask an empirical question rooted within this context: Are the causal factors for violent delinquency different from other types of juvenile crime?

As public concern over violent juvenile crime has increased, so has research data compilation. It is now common knowledge that a "violent few" account for a disproportionate percentage of violent offenses committed by juveniles (Wolfgang et al., 1972; Hamparian et al., 1978; Shannon, 1981). However, the small sample sizes in previous studies of violent youths have been a barrier to theory construction and hypothesis testing. There is little systematic information other than aggregate data on demographics, offense patterns, psychosocial characteristics, and other descriptors that distinguishes violent delinquents from other delinquents or alternatively, that differentiates types of violent offenders. For example, in a recent study of delinquency and social status (Thornberry and Farnsworth, 1981) violent offenders were excluded from the sample because of the negligible number of youths with histories of violent offenses.

What we do know is generally descriptive of both violent and nonviolent delinquents. We are all told at various times that violent youths are older youths (between 16 and 17, see Gold and Reimer, 1975); males (Strasburg, 1978); black and/or of low social status (Wolfgang et al., 1972); from broken homes (e.g., Strasburg, 1978); educational failures (e.g., Baker and Sarbin, 1965); emotionally disturbed or psychotic (e.g., Sorrells, 1977; Strasburg, 1978) gang members (e.g., Miller, 1976a, 1976b); child abuse victims (e.g., Alfaro, 1978); and from violent or poor neighborhoods (e.g., Wolfgang, 1978). Violent youths tend to victimize other youths, usually from the same or comparable neighborhoods (McDermott and Hindelang, 1981). All of these characteristics apply equally to "violent," "serious," or "chronic" delinquents, as well as to a host of other categories of youthful offenders. Generally, violent acts appear to be occasional occurrences within an overall pattern of delinquent behaviors, while a small number "specialize" in one of several offense types. Although most violent juveniles engage in a variety of delinquent behaviors, not all delinquents commit violent acts (Hamparian et al., 1978).

The wide range of causes and correlates cited above dispels single-theory explanations of violent or serious delinquency. We hypothesize that different types and patterns of delinquency require different explanations, or at least a paradigm with several causal paths, each with variably weighted factors. Recent reviews of delinquency theory and supporting research show that the current competing explanations of the causes of violent juvenile delinquency are in need of further elaboration and integration (Weis and Sederstrom, 1981). Juvenile delinquency and violent juvenile crime are complex phenomena involving interactional, individual, and environmental influences (Sadoff, 1978; Earls, 1979). Hawkins and Weis (1980), for example, reviewed ten self-reported delinquency data sets and concluded that there are multiple correlates and causes of delinquency operating within the institutional domains of family, schools, peers, and community. To the extent that any theory or set of theories fails to take into account and integrate each of these influences, its explanatory power—and thereby its usefulness—is limited.

INTEGRATED THEORY

Over the past thirty years and particularly during the past decade, a number of theories have been advanced and modified in an attempt to explain the causes of juvenile delinquency and, to a lesser extent, violence. Although there are several major schools of etiological thought, two primary thrusts dominate both past and present research. One orientation focuses primarily on the individual personality. In this view, youth become delinquent through a predisposition (physical or psychic) to delinquency or a developmental trauma. This psychogenic thrust is evident in positions that ascribe the motivation for delinquency to such causes as faulty family interaction patterns, instinctual aggressiveness, and neurological dysfunction. The second orientation stresses the contribution of social, economic, cultural, and situational factors in the development of delinquent behavior. These sociogenic theories address the correlation of high delinquency rates with rapid population mobility, minority and low-income status, and various familial characteristics such as broken homes, suicide, alcoholism, and child abuse and neglect.

There have been several attempts recently to integrate these theoretical orientations. One common interface has been between social learning theory and control theory (see Conger, 1980; Hawkins and Weis, 1980); others have integrated strain with control perspectives (Elliott and Voss, 1974). Elliott et al. (1979) have proposed a combination of the control, strain, and social learning approaches. The dynamic relationships among the variables and processes of these integrated models present opportunities to intervene with both the "causes" of delinquency (via control theory) and the manner in which these causes operate in the social development context (via social learning theory, see Hawkins and Weis, 1980).

The theoretical model of violent delinquency we propose to use integrates control, strain, and social learning perspectives of delinquent behavior (as in Elliott et al., 1979). It identifies salient factors on which to focus treatment interventions by describing the processes that govern socialization and delinquent behavior development (Hawkins and Weis, 1980) and by specifying a motivational component (Conger, 1980). The incorporation of early childhood socialization factors addresses those causal roots of violence that cannot be easily explained within prevailing delinquency theories. Thus, by specifying violence as the behavior to be studied, rather than delinquent conduct, the explanatory theory should incorporate individual psychosocial factors unique to violent youth, as well as sociological concepts associated with delinquency theory (Sorrells, 1977, 1980).

The model specifies two types of "control" bonds—integration and commitment—that are elements of socialization (Elliott et al., 1979). Integration, or external bonds, includes such variables as social roles, participation in conventional activities, and the presence of effective sanctioning networks. These variables also involve attachment to conventional groups such as the family, school, career, peers, and so on. Commitment, or internal bonds, includes such variables as conventional goals, norms, and values; personal attachment to parents and peers; social identification; and feelings of control.

Strain and learning theory focus on the processes (i.e., the specific experiences or conditions) that strengthen or weaken social bonds and allow for the "learning" of criminal values and behavior patterns as opposed to conventional values and behaviors. Attenuating processes include delinquent learning, negative reinforcement of failure experiences in conventional activities, blocked opportunities, and social disorganization at home, in school, and on the street that threatens the stability and cohesion of conventional social groups. The learning component is also informed by labeling theorists who have noted the learning involved in the assignment of a negative label (see Schur, 1973).

The theoretical model suggests that youth may become delinquent and/or violent in one of two ways. First, individual psychological factors or early childhood development experiences can precipitate outbursts of violence—the episodic dyscontrol described by Sorrells (1977, 1980). Second, youths may be "socialized" to become delinquent and/or violent. In this framework, social and personal bonds to conformity are underdeveloped or weakened, and

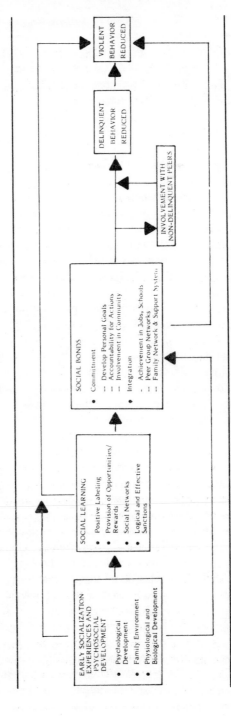

Figure 6.1   Intervention Model for Violent Juvenile Delinquency

youths are socialized (i.e., reinforced) to a delinquent lifestyle through peer influences. Hirschi (1969), in his formulation of control theory, suggests that peer influence is an important supplement to explanations of why delinquent behavior occurs when social bonds are weakened.

Social bonds develop in the units in which socialization occurs: family, school, law, and peers. If youths develop weak social bonds to schools, family, the law, or positive peers, they become free to associate with and be influenced by delinquent peers. Under such conditions, given individual factors, violent delinquency may occur. Even where youths have developed strong bonds, violence may occur as a result of childhood experiences or because the bonds they have developed are to violent peers. Social environments are important reinforcing agents that strengthen or mitigate social bonds.

Strong external bonds result from positive labeling and reinforcement through school or job achievement, involvement in activities perceived as important, and positive family interactions. Strong internal bonds develop from an effective sanctioning network, setting and attainment of personal goals, and a belief in self-determiniation and control over one's environment. The development of social and personal bonds is mediated by early socialization experiences (e.g., violence as model behavior) and psychosocial development (e.g., child-rearing practices, child abuse, family cohesion). Violence can occur either when positive social bonds are weakened and the influence of violent delinquent peers becomes the youth's primary social bond, or when learned violent behavior takes over under feelings of stress, conflict, or anger or rage. The model is graphically depicted in Figure 6.1.

The theoretical model prescribes factors on which to focus intervention: goals and opportunities, and the bonds of integration and commitment. It also prescribes a behavioral component (social learning) for intervention in the process of involvement in delinquent behavior. Finally, the inclusion of psycho-social factors introduces predisposing variables that may account for violent behavior in youths with either strong or weak bonds. Such factors include families with a history of domestic violence (Alfaro, 1978; Fagan et al., 1981) and youths who are emotionally disturbed and who lack empathy (Sorrells, 1980).

In sum, an integrated theory that addresses the special case of violent delinquency includes both psychological and sociological approaches to violent behavior. It relies on properties of both the individual and the environment to explain behavior and simultaneously identifies factors on which to focus treatment and intervention. Finally, it specifies both the factors that underlie violent delinquency and the processes by which youths may become delinquent and/or violent.

Research Questions

The integrated theory suggests several research issues. First, the relative contributions of strengthening social bonds and developing "accountability" for one's behavior to reductions in violent and nonviolent recidivism can be empirically determined. This will, in turn, shed light on the extent to which a general model of delinquency can explain violent delinquency. A second research issue is whether interventions to strengthen social bonds alone are sufficient to eliminate violence, or whether there must also be behavior-specific interventions. This issue subsumes several major research questions:

- To what extent are violent delinquents engaged in all forms of delinquency?

- What are the relative contributions of individual social structural and environmental factors to the onset and cessation of violent behavior?

- What are the relative contributions of individual factors and personal or social bonds to reduce delinquency?

- What are the potential contributions of social learning theory and practices as behavior change modalities?

Finally, the third research issue focuses on the relative importance of social (integration) and personal (commitment) bonds to nondelinquent lifestyles. If violence alone ceases but youths continue to commit delinquent acts, we might conclude that delinquency and violence are somewhat independent and are possibly "caused" by different factors. Integration and commitment may be differently affected by these interventions, thereby providing some evidence for the relative importance of social structural and attitudinal factors in delinquency and violence.

METHODS

Face-to-face interviews were conducted with 63 youths in juvenile corrections programs in four cities. Each youth had been adjudicated delinquent on one of seven target violent offenses[1] and had at least one prior adjudication for either a felonious violent offense or a serious property crime wherein a weapon was used.[2] The prior history criteria were intended to ensure that youths were chronically, not episodically, violent. Interviews were conducted by on-site researchers in each locale. The interviews took about two hours and were usually conducted in two parts. Youths were paid $10 for participation regardless of whether the interview was completed. These youths were participants in a federally sponsored research and development program testing an intervention model based on the theory described in the preceeding section. They were identified for the study after adjudicatory proceedings and then randomly assigned and placed in experimental or control programs.

Interview schedules included explanatory variables corresponding to the theory discussed above. Items were designed to solicit information on the youth's delinquent involvement, family relations and environment, attitudes toward the law and violence, education and work achievement, personal goals, crime victimization, drug use, school and neighborhood environment, peer relations, and peer delinquency. Additive scales were developed to reflect the component concepts of integration and commitment, including such domains as school, work, peer, and family. Social learning variables were reflected in several environmental factors (e.g., peer delinquency, school environment, family violence, family normlessness). The Brief Symptom Inventory, or BSI (Derogatis et al., 1973), a standardized psychological inventory measuring emotional disturbance, was also used to measure the psychosocial domain. A complete listing of scales is available on request from the authors.

Delinquency measures included 32 self-reported delinquency (SRD) items similar to those employed in the National Youth Survey (NYS), a longitudinal study of delinquency and drug use among American youth from 1976 to 1980 (Elliott et al., 1981). The SRD items ask respondents to indicate if they had ever committed each offense, and if so, how many times during the last 12 months. Four scales measuring drug, property, force or violence, and general delinquency were constructed for each of the response sets ("ever" and "how often"). The "ever" scales were derived by summing the reported scores for the separate offense items included in each delinquency scale; these scales measure the number of types of offenses committed by each youth within the drug, property, and force or violence categories as well as the total. The second set of scales were constructed to estimate the most recent delinquent behaviors by summing the frequencies for each subset of offenses. These scales are termed "recency".

The analyses are designed to provide a preliminary test of a theoretical model of violent delinquency. The analyses attempt to answer such questions as "What are the more important factors within and across domains contributing to different types of delinquency?" The analyses also examine the relationship between individual and environmental factors and behavioral patterns. We began our analysis by examining the correlations between the theoretically constructed scales and the violence, property, drug, and total delinquency scales. The violence scale includes 13 items covering a spectrum of activities ranging from threatened to actual violence. The scale includes such items as threaten an adult, hit a teacher, beat up someone so badly it resulted in serious injury, using a weapon, and killing someone. The mean number of types of violent crime is 4.6. The drug scale consists of five items addressing the use of alcohol and drugs, the sale of drugs, and activities done while high or loaded. The mean number of activities ever engaged in is 1.63 and the standard deviation is 1.5. Therefore, the majority of youth in our sample have engaged in a substance abuse-related activity. The property crime scale includes 13 offenses ranging from damaging property to stealing it from family, school, or strangers. The youth in our sample committed an average of 4.6 types of property crime in their lifetime. The total scale is additive of the above three scales with a possible 31 types of crimes. The mean number of categories of crime committed in total is 10.7, with a standard deviation of 6.6.

In order to explore these relationships within each domain, stepwise regression analysis was performed to determine the overall variance explained in each regression model and to evaluate the relative contribution of specific scales to delinquency. For those variables whose change in R^2 is greater than .02, the bivariate relationships between delinquency outcome and the independent variables were examined within domains using contigency table analysis. The gamma scores are reported for the bivariate relationships.

The small sample size (N = 63) qualifies the interdomain analyses. Subsequent analyses of these data will permit larger explanatory variable sets to be analyzed, and findings will be interpreted with greater confidence. This will lead to more thorough examination of the more global concepts of integration, commitment, social learning, and psychosocial factors. Also, larger samples will make it possible to compute path analyses to test alternative ordering of variables as they contribute to violent delinquency.

Finally, readers should bear in mind that the sample in this study is composed exclusively of chronically violent delinquents. The use of SRD scales to measure three types of delinquent behaviors among this population acknowledges the fact that such youths commit a wide range of offenses, not all of which are violent. This study, then, attempts to address shortcomings in previous research where the causes and internal structures of violent delinquency were inferred based on differences in explanatory variables between often large nonviolent delinquent and very small violent delinquent populations. By closely examining a range of offense and behavior patterns among a homogeneous population, we hope to describe more sensitively the population and identify the internal linkages and interrelationships among the variables associated with three types of violent delinquents.

RESULTS

SRD Scales

Table 6.1 shows the item distributions for SRD scales for both Ever and Recency scales. The results for each scale demonstrate the wide range of behaviors in which chronically violent youths are involved. For each scale, the frequency of a given act decreases with its severity

Despite the sample of chronically violent youths, we observed none of the extremely high frequencies for some of the more serious or violent offenses that were found in the NYS results (Elliott et al., 1981). Moreover, these data may seriously underestimate the prevalence of some types of violence among these youths. Despite only one self-report of "forced sex," official records revealed four youths in this sample who were adjudicated for rape. Eight youths in this sample were adjudicated delinquent for murder, yet only three reported "killing someone." Overall, however, the general trend and distributions of these items and scales is consistent with an analysis of official records for the same youths (Hartstone et al., 1982).

Table 6.2 shows the correlation matrix for each SRD scale and the Ever and Recency scales. The high intrascale coefficients are all significant at the .01 level and offer interesting insights into the career offense patterns. Each Ever scale is highly correlated with its respective Recency scale, indicating that if a youth ever engaged in a type of delinquency, there is high likelihood that he also engaged in that behavior in the past year. The Total-Recency scale is highly correlated with all three Ever scales. The Property-Ever scale shows somewhat lower correlations with the Recency scales than the three other Ever scales. Overall, the relatively strong correlations support the picture of the versatile offender in these data as elsewhere (e.g., Rojek and Erickson, 1982).

There is some evidence here, however, that if a youth's violence is more extensive (that is, if he committed a greater number of violent acts in the past), he is likely to have a greater number of recent violent acts. On the other hand, where past career is more property oriented, the likelihood of recent violence decreases. These data are consistent with past prediction studies that indicate that prior violence is the most reliable indicator of subsequent violence (e.g., Monahan, 1977, 1980), and that while not specializing, some youths certainly emphasize violent delinquency. This certainly is no argument for a theory of offense specialization among violent youths, but it does suggest that some youths are more violent than others; in particular their total career is more oriented toward violent crime.

Given these results, we next decided to focus on the SRD-Ever scales, a set of dichotomous variables, for model testing and specification. Table 6.3 shows the SRD scale correlations. Together with Table 6.2 these data suggest that youths in this study have engaged in a domain of behaviors that is quite consistent and identifiable. Although Total Violence has the highest correlation ($r = .87$), the

TABLE 6.1 Self-Reports of Delinquent Acts by VJO Respondents

| | | | Frequency Within Last Year | | | | | |
| | Ever | | Less than Once a Month | | 1-3 Times a Month | | Once a Week or More | |
	N	(%)*	N	(%)	N	(%)	N	(%)
Alcohol and drug-related item (Drug)								
Drank liquor	31	(49)	15	(24)	5	(8)	11	(17)
Attended school high	29	(46)	19	(30)	1	(2)	9	(14)
Used illegal drugs	25	(40)	15	(24)	3	(5)	7	(11)
Drove car while high	18	(29)	12	(19)	3	(5)	3	(5)
Sold illegal drugs	7	(27)	9	(14)	2	(3)	6	(10)
Property-related items (Property)								
Sold stolen goods	48	(76)	32	(51)	7	(11)	9	(14)
Bought stolen goods	37	(59)	31	(49)	2	(3)	4	(6)
Damaged other property	34	(54)	30	(48)	3	(5)	1	(3)
Broken into building to steal	29	(46)	24	(38)	3	(5)	2	(3)
Broken into a car	23	(36)	20	(32)	1	(2)	2	(3)
Taken goods from store	22	(35)	18	(29)	2	(3)	2	(3)

Taken something from a purse	22	(35)	18	(29)	3	(5)	1	(2)
Stolen at school	19	(30)	18	(29)	–	–	1	(2)
Damaged school property	15	(24)	15	(24)	–	–	–	–
Taken a car	23	(36)	19	(30)	2	(3)	2	(3)
Damaged family property	15	(24)	14	(22)	–	–	1	(2)
Grabbed a purse and ran	14	(22)	14	(22)	–	–	–	–
Stolen money from family	8	(13)	7	(11)	1	(2)	–	–
Force/Violence-related delinquency **(Violence)**								
Carried weapon	43	(68)	34	(59)	1	(3)	8	(13)
Pulled weapon	33	(52)	26	(41)	4	(6)	3	(5)
Threatened an adult	36	(57)	31	(49)	2	(3)	3	(5)
Used weapon	32	(51)	26	(41)	3	(5)	3	(5)
Beat someone until injured	33	(52)	28	(44)	2	(3)	3	(5)
Threatened an adult with weapon	33	(52)	27	(43)	4	(6)	2	(3)
Threatened to hurt	28	(44)	22	(35)	2	(3)	4	(6)
Hit a teacher	19	(30)	19	(30)	–	–	–	–
Used physical force	20	(32)	14	(22)	4	(6)	2	(3)
Shot someone	15	(24)	15	(24)	–	–	–	–
Killed someone	3	(5)	3	(5)	–	–	–	–
Hit a parent	3	(5)	2	(3)	1	(2)	–	–
Forced someone to have sex	1	(2)	1	(2)	–	–	–	–

*Percentage based on total number of 63.

TABLE 6.2   Correlation Coefficients Between Ever and
Recency SRD Scales

| Ever | Recency (Frequency in Past Year) | | | |
	Drug	Property	Violence	Total
Drug	.86	.53	.48	.70
Property	.43	.80	.38	.64
Violence	.61	.52	.80	.79
Total	.71	.75	.67	.85

others are also high and show behavior patterns in terms of overall careers that are nearly indistinguishable.

Finally, Table 6.4 shows the correlation matrix for the SRD scales with the theoretical variables. The sample size is 63 except where noted. Overall, the SRD scales share common relationships with many explanatory variables. However, several notable variations exist. The explanatory sets for property and violence have several important distinctions. Among family variables, for example, family violence is associated with violence, but not property crime. Conversely, weak family attachments are negatively associated with property only. Among school variables, School Integration, an individual-level variable, is negatively associated with all outcomes, but a significant relationship exists only with property. School delinquency (an environmental variable) is associated only with violence. Peer influence is strong for both scales. The main difference is that peer integration and the number of peer contacts with juvenile justice system are significantly associated with violence and not with property. The major difference between the two SRD scales in the work domain is the role of Work Quality-Opportunity. Although the association is negative for all scales, it is not significant for property crimes. Work opportunities are associated with a decrease in violent crime but not in property crime.

Two different variables are significantly associated with Property and Violence, respectively. Victimization, a scale measuring the extent to which youth in the sample had ever been victims of a serious property or violent offense, is positively correlated with Property. The more an individual is a victim of crime, the more likely he is to commit property offenses but not violent offenses. Self-Improvement is negatively correlated with Property. The more an individual strives to achieve personal goals (e.g., hold down a job, develop strong friendships, make a good life for himself), the fewer property crimes he commits. This supports the hypothesis that developing social bonds (which reflects being invested in society and its possible rewards) is associated with committing fewer crimes. Not surprisingly, violence is associated with accepting attitudes toward violence as an integral part of life. Espousing attitudes that reflect law-abiding principles are negatively associated with violence, also an

TABLE 6.3 Intercorrelations of Self-Reported Delinquency Scales-Ever

	Property	*Violence*	*Total*
Drug	.49	.55	.75
Property	–	.56	.85
Violence	–	–	.87

expected finding. What is interesting, however, is that the relationship is significant with Violence and not the other SRD scales.

One finding that is less clear in its implications is the significant positive correlation between locus of control and violence. The Locus of Control variable is a composite of beliefs that one has control over one's life. For example, it includes agreeing with statements such as, "When I make plans, I'm almost certain that I can make them work" or disagreeing with, "For me, good luck is more important than hard work for success." The reason this finding is significant only for Violence, and correlates in a positive direction, continues to mystify us.

Multivariate Analyses

Table 6.5 shows the multivariate relationship of the explanatory variables to each SRD score, within each theoretical domain. The variables included are those that contribute at least 2% of the variance explained in the regression analyses. Each of these variables was subsequently cross-tabulated with the criterion variable, and the gamma statistics are reported.

Family. Family Normlessness, a measure of family members' contact with the law, is consistently the strongest predictor of the SRD outcomes. Only the gamma score for the Drug outcome indicates a strong association. Family Violence, an indicator of physical fighting between parents and among siblings, has a strong effect on the Violence scale, but its gamma (.40) is not statistically significant. Family Attachment is a weak predictor of each scale. The gamma scores are all negative but not significant. Family Involvement is also a weak predictor.

School. Only two school variables were entered into regression equations. The first, School Delinquency, is an additive scale of all types of behavior reported by the youth to be done by fellow students at school. The second, School Integration, is a composite of the youth's attitudes toward teachers and grades, effort, attendance, and satisfaction. The third school variable, School Behavior, is autocorrelated with the SRD outcome scales and was excluded. For the Drug, Violence and Total SRD scales, Schools Delinquency is the strongest predictor, with consistently strong associations with each of the scales except Property. While having a negative impact on each of the scales (except Violence where the gamma is not reported), School Integration is a strong and significant predictor only of Drug crimes.

Peers. Among peer variables, peer influence at the environmental level contributes most to all outcome scales. Peer Delinquency, an additive scale of

TABLE 6.4   Correlation Coefficients Between Theoretical Variables and Self-Report Delinquency Scales

	SRD Scales			
Theoretical Scales	*Drugs*	*Property Crime*	*Violence*	*Total*
Family				
Family Normlessness	.39**	.29**	.25*	.36**
Family Violence	.02	.20	.27*	.22*
Mother Authoritarian	.16	−.03	.08	.07
Father Authoritarian	.16	.02	.11	.10
Family Social Isolation	.13	.15	.05	.13
Family Attachment	−.05	−.21*	−.13	−.17
Family Involvement	.03	−.16	−.10	−.11
School				
School Integration[1]	−.33**	−.33**	−.24	−.35*
School Behavior[1]	.61**	.48**	.71**	.70**
School Delinquency[1]	.30*	.17	.48**	.38**
Peers				
Peer Integration	.26*	.16	.39**	.32**
Peer Delinquency	.58**	.37**	.44**	.53**
Confidante's Violence	.30**	.49**	.38**	.48**
Advice Seeker's Violence	.21*	.34**	.38**	.39**
Peer Contact w/JJS (ever)	.33**	.28**	.28**	.35**
Peer Contact w/JJS (#)	.23**	.20	.36**	.32**
Work				
Work Integration[2]	−.38**	−.34**	−.26*	−.41**
Work Delinquency[2]	.01	.09	.04	.07
Work Quality/Opportunity[2]	−.39**	−.28	−.37**	−.44**
Social Relations-Attitudes				
Attitudes toward Violence	.27*	.12	.41**	.32**
Victimization	.25*	.51**	.14	.37**
Personal Goals	.07	.14	.06	.11
Lack of money	.16	.14	.19	.20
Self-Improvement	−.13	−.31**	−.06	−.20
Law-Abiding	−.12	−.05	−.26*	−.18
Locus of Control	.04	−.10	.23*	.07

(continued)

TABLE 6.4 Continued

| | | SRD Scales | | |
Theoretical Scales	Drugs	Property Crime	Violence	Total
Psychosocial				
Somatization	−.16	−.03	−.11	−.11
Obsessive-Compulsive	−.02	.05	.03	.03
Interpersonal Sensitivity	−.03	.10	.09	.08
Depression	−.06	.08	.04	.04
Anxiety	.01	.13	.05	.08
Hostility	.01	.24*	.34**	.27*
Phobic Anxiety	−.10	.09	.09	.06
Paranoid Ideation	−.08	.16	.13	.11
Psychoticism	−.11	.13	.02	.04
Positive Symptom Index	−.26*	−.09	−.03	−.13
Semantic Differential	.09	.07	.04	.07
Global Severity Index	−.02	.13	.09	.08

*$p \leqslant .05$
**$p \leqslant .01$
1. $N = 45$
2. $N = 43$

delinquent activities of friends, is the strongest predictor of Drug and Violence outcomes. The variable measuring the violent behavior (crimes against persons) of the youth's confidants, Confidant's Violence, is the strongest predictor of property crimes, and is also significantly related to the Property, Violence, and Total scales. In contrast, Advice Seeker's Violence is statistically significant only in relation to the Violence scale.

The findings for the peer domain suggest that serious and violent delinquency are associated with the influence of delinquent peers at both the individual and the group level. The youth in this sample have close friends (confidants and those who seek advice) who are violent and are members of delinquent peer groups. In addition, these peer relationships appear to be influential.

Work. Work Quality-Opportunity is the strongest predictor of the prevalence of each type of delinquency, with the exception of property crimes. Both regression analyses and cross-tabulations show that where working youths perceive growth, benefits, and tangible rewards from their employment, they commit fewer of each type of offense. Work Delinquency, or the extent to which co-workers commit delinquent acts, is a weak contributor to each SRD scale. Work Integration, or the extent of a youths' attachment to and involvement in the workplace, also has negligible effects but has strong, negative gammas (although not significant).

TABLE 6.5   Multivariate Analyses for Each Domain and
Bivariate Relationships with SRD Scales

	Drug		Property		Violence		Total	
	ΔR^2	Gamma	ΔR^2	Gamma	ΔR^2	Gamma	ΔR^2	Gamma
Family								
Family Normlessness	.15	.50*	.10	.16	.03	.19	.13	.18
Family Violence	–	–	–	–	.08	.40	–	–
Family Attachment	–	–	.08	-.40	.02	-.10	.06	-.13
Family Involvement	.02	-.18	–	–	–	–	–	–
School								
School Delinquency	.04	.59*	–	–	.23	.45**	.14	.42*
School Integration	.11	-.67*	.11	-.62	–	–	.06	-.51
Peers								
Peer Delinquency	.34	.76**	.06	.45	.19	.58**	.28	.65**
Peer Integration	.03	.16	–	–	.11	.33	.03	.20
Confidante's Violence	–	–	.24	.56*	.02	.58*	.12	.49**
Advice Seeker's Violence	–	–	–	–	.04	.49**	–	–
Work								
Work Quality-Opportunity	.15	-.46*	–	–	.15	-.66**	.19	-.69**
Work Delinquency	.02	–	.04	–	.02	–	.04	–
Work Integration	.03	-.47	.12	-.53	–	–	.04	-.67*
Social Relations-Attitudes								
Attitudes Towards Violence	.06	.10	–	–	.18	.34	.11	.22
Personal Goals	–	–	.02	.28	–	–	–	–
Law Abiding Attitudes	–	–	–	–	.04	-.10	.02	.06
Efforts to Achieve Goals	–	–	.10	-.34	–	–	.02	-.34
Psychosocial								
PSDI	.07	-.56	.09	-.36	.09	-.16	.13	-.33
Locus of Control	–	–	–	–	.06	.04	–	–
Interpersonal Sensitivity	–	–	–	–	–	–	–	–
Hostility	.03	.17	.08	.24	.12	.63**	.08	.37

*$p \leq .05$
**$p \leq .01$

Social relations and attitudes. A range of variables were examined that
measure social attitudes toward the law and violence, as well as personal
activities such as goal setting and planned efforts to achieve personal goals.
These scales are components of the concept of "commitment" (Elliott et al.,
1979) in this integrated theory.

The results are varied and largely inconclusive. Only Personal Goals (e.g., do
well in school, hold down a job, have self-respect, develop strong friendships)
and Efforts to Achieve Goals (improve education, learn skills, etc.) contribute
to the explained variance in Property. For the Violence and Total outcomes,
Attitudes Toward Violence is the strongest predictor; it includes agreement with
statements such as , "It's OK to hit someone to get them to do what you want"
or "If you don't physically fight back, people will walk all over you." Law-
Abiding Attitudes is a weak (negative) contributor, as was expected; it includes
disagreement with items such as, "It's all right to get around the law if you can

get away with it" and "Everybody steals something once in a while." Interestingly, Attitudes Toward Violence is the strongest contributor to all SRD scales (with the exception of Property) for the explanatory domain. None of the bivariate relationships was statistically significant.

Psychosocial factors. Regression analyses for each SRD scale were conducted with the BSI scales plus Locus of Control (a measure of the youth's feelings of control over his future and well-being). Although no contributions to variance explained are noteworthy, one significant association was observed: an expected relationship between the BSI Hostility scale and Violence. This is not surprising, given that a natural response to a hostile environment is the use of hostile personal defenses.

Victimization. Victimization shows strong and significant correlations with all SRD scales except Violence. This varible is a 9-item additive scale measuring the extent to which repondents had ever been victims of a serious property or violent offenses. It is an indicator of the extent to which the youth has been personally affected by serious crime, and we interpret it as a measure of the youth's environment. We did not include it in any of the regressions described above, as it did not fit easily into the domains delineated within the theoretical model. However, because of its high correlation coefficients, we examined the cross-tabulations of Victimization with each SRD scale. The results are shown in Table 6.6. Only Property is significantly associated with Victimization, and the association is strong (gamma = .74). Being victimized appears to increase the likelihood that a youth will engage in behaviors and crimes similar to those perpetrated on him.

Interdomain Analyses

The integrated theory suggests that explanatory variables from several domains will contribute to violent delinquency, but it does not specify an ordering of the contributions or their relative importance. To examine this question, multiple regression analyses were undertaken to examine the relationships among both environmental influences and individual (control) factors across the domains of peers, school, employment, family, and neighborhood. As in earlier intradomain analyses (Table 6.5), we report only those variables that contribute at least 2% of the variance explained in the regression, and also the bivariate relationships of these variables to the four SRD scales.

One limitation on these analyses is the small number of subjects with both work and school experiences (N = 27). It was not possible to analyze the joint effects of these domains at either the environmental or the individual level. Therefore, separate analyses in Tables 6.7.and 6.8 were conducted for work and school contributions with the other domains.

Environmental factors. Table 6.7 shows the results of multiple regression equations predicting the SRD scales from five environmental variables. The predictive power of these equations is substantial, explaining from 46% to 60%

TABLE 6.6   Self-Reported Delinquency by Victimization

		Victimization			
		Low	Medium	High	
SRD Property	Low	14 (88)	10 (62)	9 (29)	33 (52)
	High	2 (12)	6 (38)	22 (81)	30 (48)
		16	16	31	63

$\chi^2 = 15.3$; $p \leqslant .01$; gamma = .74

		Victimization			
		Low	Medium	High	
SRD Violence	Low	10 (62)	7 (44)	14 (45)	31 (49)
	High	6 (38)	9 (56)	17 (55)	32 (51)
		16	16	31	63

$\chi^2 = 1.52$; n.s.; gamma = .20

of the variance. An exception is the Violence scale for work variables, with 30% of the variance explained.

The first set of equations includes work variables. The strongest predictor for each SRD scale in this set is different. For Drug use, Peer Delinquency is the strongest predictor. For Property, Victimization is the strongest. Work Quality-Opportunity is the strongest predictor of Violence and Total delinquency. Again, where youths have had positive work experiences (i.e., earn money, have job satisfaction, see opportunity for advancement), Violence is lowest.

Looking across SRD scales for each domain, we see that Work Quality-Opportunity shows consistently strong bivariate associations with all scales (though not necessarily significant). It also is a strong predictor of Violence and Total. Peer Delinquency is strongly associated with all scales except Property. Victimization is associated only with Property and Total. Finally, Intimate's Violence is also a strong contributor to Total delinquency. This scale combines two previous scales: Confidant's Violence and Advice Seeker's Violence.[3] The most consistent of the family variables, Family Normlessness—surprisingly—is a negligible contributor to all scales.

TABLE 6.7   Interdomain Multivariate Analyses and Bivarate Relationships Using Environmental-Level Predictors

	Drugs		Property		Violence		Total	
	ΔR^2	Gamma	ΔR^2	Gamma	ΔR^2	Gamma	ΔR^2	Gamma
Environmental Factors (with work variables, N = 43)								
Peer Delinquency	.34	.76**	—	—	.03	.58**	.06	.65**
Work Quality-Opportunity	.08	−.46*	.03	−.47	.15	−.66**	.18	−.69**
Family Normlessness	.02	.50*	.09	.16	—	—	—	—
Victimization	.02	.35	.38	.74**	—	—	.06	.48**
Intimate's Violence	—	—	.02	.54*	.12	.62**	.22	.59**
Environmental Factors (with school variables, N = 45)								
Peer Delinquency	.44	.76**	.14	.45	.23	.58**	.36	.65**
Family Normlessess	.06	.50*	—	—	.02	.19	—	—
School Delinquency	.04	.59*	—	—	.11	.45**	.04	.42*
Victimization	—	—	.08	.74**	—	—	.02	.48**
Intimate's Violence	—	—	.28	.52*	.17	.62**	.18	.59**

*p ≤ .05
**p ≤ .01

When School Delinquency is substituted for Work Quality, the results shift. The strongest predictors of all SRD scales are either one or both: Intimate's Violence and Peer Delinquency. Also, Victimization is again associated with Property offenses. School Delinquency, a measure of the extent of delinquency in the youth's school, is a strong predictor only of Violence, although it is significantly associated with Drug and Total scales. Interestingly, it does not enter the equation for Property crimes.

These results suggest that different domains contribute in different ways to the SRD scales. Peer Delinquency is the strongest predictor among this environmental set, of all types of delinquency except Property. Family Normlessness is not a major factor for youths in school or at work. Intimate's Violence is significantly associated with Property, Violence, and Total outcomes and is a major predictor of Property crime (with school variables). Victimization is a strong predictor of Property crimes for both youths in school and those with work experience. Finally, both work opportunities and school environment are notable predictors of Violence, but not Property, outcomes.

Individual predictors. Table 6.8 shows the results of parallel analysis of individual-level (or control theory) variables from family, school, peer, and work domains. These variables were selected for inclusion from Table 6.5 as the strongest individual-level intradomain predictors. Again, two sets of equations were computed, one each with work and school variables. The percentage of variance explained here is much lower than with the environmental level variables: R^2 ranges from .15 to .37.

TABLE 6.8   Interdomain Multivariate Analyses and Bivariate Relationships Using Individual-Level Predictors

	Drugs		Property		Violence		Total	
	ΔR^2	Gamma	ΔR^2	Gamma	ΔR^2	Gamma	ΔR^2	Gamma
Individual Factors (with work variables, N = 43)								
Work Integration	.14	−.47	.12	−.53	.04	−.49	.16	−.67**
Attitudes Toward Violence	.04	.10	−	−	.17	.34	.05	.22
Family Attachment	−	−	.03	−.40	.04	−.10	−	−
Family Involvement	−	−	−	−	−	−	−	−
Peer Integration	−	−	−	−	−	−	−	−
Individual Factors (with school variables, N = 45)								
School Integration	.11	−.67*	.11	−.62	.05	−.38	.11	−.51
Peer Integration	.08	.16	.06	.45	.30	.33	.20	.20
Attitudes Toward Violence	.02	.10	−	−	.02	.34	−	−
Family Attachment	−	−	−	−	−	−	−	−
Family Involvement	−	−	.05	−.33	−	−	−	−

*p ≤ .05
**p ≤ .01

The first set includes work variables. Overall, few variables are both strong predictors and significantly associated with the outcomes. Work integration is the stongest predictor of Drug outcomes, and also contributes to Total delinquency. It is negatively associated with each of the outcomes, but the relationship is significant only with Total. Attitudes Toward Violence is the stonger predictor of Violence, but its bivariate relationship is weak and not statistically significant. Family variables are neither strong predictors of, nor significantly associated with, any of the SRD scales. Peer Integration made no contribution over 2% of the explained variance to each of the outcomes.

When School Integration is included as an explanatory variable (as opposed to Work Integration), the results shift. School Integration is significantly associated only with the Drug scale. Peer Integration is the strongest predictor of Violence and Total. The combination of Peer Integration and School Integration appears to be the main influence for individual-level variables. As with individual work factors, family variables remain uninfluential, as do Attitudes Toward Violence.

Comparison of Individual and Environmental Predictors

Although the sample size for this analysis is small and the multivariate findings must be regarded cautiously, a comparison between the individual- and environmental-level analyses can be made. The most striking contrast between Tables 6.7 and 6.8 is the generally stronger explanatory power of the environmental variables—these variables explain from 30% to 60% of the variance for each SRD scale while the individual-level variables explain 15% to 37%. This imbalance in explanatory power between individual-level and environmental-level regressions dictates caution in generalizing the effects of any particular domain. Aggregate contrasts across levels and domains are cautiously undertaken here.

The first important contrast is between work and school variables. For youths in school, there is consistency of explanatory factors across offense type. This is generally true for both environmental and individual variable sets. School and Peer Delinquency and Integration are consistently the most powerful combination of variables. Intimate's Violence, a more intense peer influence, is also a powerful environmental influence. Clearly peer and school influences provides a fertile learning ground for delinquency.

For youths who work, there is less consistency: Different explanatory variables explain different offense types. For example, at the environmental level, Victimization is the most powerful predictor of Property crime, while Work Quality-Opportunity and Intimate's Violence were the strongest in explaining Violence. At the individual level, Work Integration is the strongest predictor (although weak overall) in explaining everything except Violence. Work environments are made up of a complex set of social and interpersonal influences. Employment appears to minimize the influence of peers and expose youth to different norms, rules, and socializing influences, as well as offering new opportunities. The importance of peers cannot be overstated. But as is clear in the above analysis, they are much more influential for those youth who are not employed.[4]

The comparative analysis also suggests the uniqueness of Violence relative to the other types of crime. The integrated theory hypothesized that violence was a different type of crime, and our analysis does not disconfirm that. For the explanatory set with work variables included, Violence is predicted by factors different from other offense types. When school variables are substituted for work variables, Violence is no longer uniquely predicted. Violence among youths in school may be qualitatively different phenomenon than violence among working youth and certainly appears to be shaped and influenced by different environmental forces. This finding thus supports the contention that it is useful to study violent behavior apart from general delinquency.

A third notable finding is the powerful role of Intimate's Violence. In the environmental-level analysis, it emerges as a predictor for both work and school variable sets. This is not surprising. Intimates include family as well as friends and can be influential independent of any particular environment. It appears to be a more intense form of both peer and family influence, as well as more specifically focused on reinforcement violence, not delinquency.

Finally, these two tables are noteworthy in the relative absence of familial influence. Families, despite their structural configuration, contact with the law or internal violence, do not play a major role in either facilitating or inhibiting violent delinquency.

SUMMARY AND DISCUSSION

Social policy for delinquent youths has shifted dramatically in recent years from the rehabilitative ideals of the juvenile court to the punitive and incapacitative approach of the adult court. This shift is due in large part to the small but difficult population of violent delinquents and perceived failure to develop effective treatment programs to control and reintegrate these youths. A philosophy of retribution and punishment has replaced the rehabilitative ideal, based on a widely held belief that nothing works: Programs don't rehabilitate, and they cannot balance public protection with the ideals of treatment. This shift in delinquency policy suggests that the causes of crime are too complex to be addressed through social policy.

Prior research has not adequately addressed the causes of violent delinquency because of both methodological difficulties and inadequate theory. Previous studies that attempted to determine the causes of violent juvenile crime have relied on large sample sizes to measure the differences among violent youths, other delinquents, and nondelinquent youths. Because so few youths are chronically violent, these studies cannot confidently make such discriminations. Theoretical research has generally failed to test integrated models that include factors and processes indentified in previous studies but that alone fail to explain violent delinquency.

This research effort addresses these problems by testing an integrated theory of violent delinquency on a homogeneous sample of chronically violent youths who met stringent criteria for inclusion in the study. The theoretical model specifies the characteristics of violent youths and hypothesizes the processes by which they become violent. It includes both sociological and psychological factors that operate at the individual and environmental level.

Patterns of Violent Delinquency

Self-reported delinquency (SRD) data show that violent youths report a wide range of offenses, including drug and property crimes as well as violent crimes. Although youths do not specialize in one behavior or another, some of these youths appear to be more violent. Youths whose careers include more property offenses appear less violent in the recent past, while youths with more violent overall careers appear to commit more violent crimes at the time of interview.

While there is little evidence here to support offense specialization theories, these data suggest that we may be asking the wrong questions in typifying delinquent careers of violent youths. In the past, criminologists have generally studied delinquent conduct without specifying violence. Other disciplines (e.g., psychology) have tended to emphasize the study of violence. However, the data here suggest that this dichotomy is ill-conceived: Violent youth also commit nonviolent offenses, while other delinquent youths are totally nonviolent. The data here suggest that attempts to develop taxonomies of delinquent careers should incorporate both overall career pattern and the recency of a particular type of offense. That is, a more sensitive index of delinquent career would include both temporal (i.e., recency) and severity dimensions of criminality.

Testing the Integrated Theory

To test the integrated theory of violent delinquency, four self-report delinquency scales were developed to explore the different offense patterns among violent youths. We identified correlates of all types of offense patterns and then examined which explanatory variables were associated with different offense patterns.

Overall, environmental variables are generally the strongest correlates of each offense pattern. Multivariate analyses also show the importance of environmental factors as contributors to overall offense patterns both within and across domains. Different offense patterns are explained by different domains of variables. Environmental factors were consistently and strongly associated with all delinquency scales, especially Violence and Drug crimes, confirming the primacy of social learning processes in this integrated theory. Control theory (or individual-level) variables do not appear to be influential contributors to self-reported delinquency, both within and across domains.

The differential contributions of individual and environmental variables can be interpreted as confirmation of the need for a complex theory to reflect the real world accurately. The complexity of the integrated theory makes it sensitive to different levels of factors that shape and influence behavior in an urban environment. Certainly the finding that Violence generally has a different set of predictors than other SRD scales lends support to the idea that different types of offenses require differing explanations.

Recall that the entire sample is composed of violent delinquents, and that the more violent among them are influenced by different factors than are those who are more involved in property offenses. It is possible that there are qualitative differences in violent behavior that account for the different explanatory factors. Violence accompanied by property crime may have different motivational basis than violence alone. Studies of aggression and violent crime have noted that expressive, rather than instrumental, violence is found among different profiles of individuals. Future analyses in this research will examine such hypotheses.

These results also suggest that an integrated model of violent delinquency can discriminate both causal and mediating factors associated with different career patterns among violent delinquents. There are different sets of explanatory factors for each offense pattern, suggesting that youths who emphasize violence differ in causal paths from youths who are only randomly or occasionally violent. Peer influence appears to be a strong predictor of violence, especially at the environmental level. Family influences are minimal overall.

Victimization—the extent to which youth is a victim of violence and property crime—was significantly associated only with property offenses. Psychosocial factors are generally weakly correlated with self-reported delinquency. One exception, however, is the individual psychological factor—hostility—which is a statistically significant correlate of more violent careers.

Self-reported delinquency appears to be shaped and reinforced through environmental influences from peers, neighborhoods, and schools. The workplace is revealed to reduce or reverse some of these effects. We cannot yet state which factors are direct influences versus mediating variables, nor can we identify interaction effects or temporal ordering. A more highly evolved and specified learning model awaits a larger sample and a more controlled design.

POLICY IMPLICATIONS

The policy implications, however, are fairly clear. We can argue, albeit tentatively, that we do indeed know something about the causes of violent juvenile crime. Public policy can address the causes by establishing a knowledge base on which programs and strategies can be built. Policy must be preventive and address the social environments that shape and influence youth. These environments condition the influences of families and peers by providing few avenues for success or law-abiding behavior. Once subject to the contingencies of poor housing and violent schools or neighborhoods, violence is quickly and understandably learned. Those youths with emotional or individual problems are subject to environmental influences, which may further reinforce problematic behaviors. Youths afforded the opportunity to associate only with violent peers or families with extensive violence or contact with the law are more likely to become delinquent and/or violent.

Specific policies to prevent serious and violent deliquency should address four areas. First, community development strategies should focus on strengthening informal social controls to reduce criminal victimization and creation of alternatives to the current Hobson's choice[5] in inner-city America. Youths comprising this study sample identified few lifesttyle choices in their neighborhoods other than criminal activity or idleness. The choice of criminal activity in that setting is reinforced both by victimization and the generally low level of negative sanctioning. Violence appears to be a rational choice in a violent setting.

Second, reducing school violence and delinquency can have a similar effect. School violence not only reinforces violent behavior among youths and peers, but it poisons the learning environment and minimizes opportunities for educational success and positive peer relationships. It reduces choices for youths and creates opportunities for victimization which, in turn, reinforce delinquency. Reductions in school violence can reverse the processes and make the school a more positive setting for education.

Third, family violence prevention strategies should also be developed. Although domestic violence did not emerge as a strong predictor in the interdomain regression analyses, it was a significant correlate of the Violence and Total SRD scales. Violence learned in the home, either through victimization or witnessing wife or sibling abuse, is associated with a violent crime in adulthood (Fagan et al., 1982). Prevention strategies can affect violent crime by both negatively portraying violence and teaching nonviolent methods of communication and conflict resolution.

Finally, salient job opportunities should be created for youth. The results here suggest that youth employment per se does not reduce delinquency. Rather, the *quality* of work opportunity (i.e., status, skills, promotion, wages) can affect all types of delinquency. This finding suggests that the wisdom of classic delinquency-opportunity theories lies in the reinforcing quality of work, rather than as a causal link (e.g., Cloward and Ohlin, 1960). Of course, youth employment policy has resisted both legislative solution and even the heartiest of economic upturns. The wisdom of current policy efforts—the elimination of both the minimum wage and child labor laws to increase youth employability—is without empirical support, and could prove to be counterproductive given the potential impact on the quality of working conditions and opportunities.

Where environmental norms are changed and more positive contingencies reinforced, violent delinquency is likely to be reduced, regardless of individual factors. Elliott et al. (1981) concluded that changes in environmental norms are the key to reduction in all types of delinquency. Our finding on work quality-opportunity is a powerful example of a potential inhibitor of violent delinquency. By providing a strong and positive environment that offers rewards and opportunities—in other words, an environment that strengthens integration—delinquency can be reduced. Such opportunities and interactions are critical components of a social policy that would reduce violent delinquency.

NOTES

1. Murder, aggravated assault, armed robbery, rape or sodomy, kidnap, arson of an occupied dwelling.

2. A complete listing of offenses is available from the authors.

3. This scale measures the extent of "person" offenses committed by people closest to the youth—those who seek his advice and those whose advice he seeks. It appears to be a powerful environmental influence. The scale is not additive of the two previous scales. Rather, if either of the respective scales had affirmative responses, the results were incorporated into the new scale.

4. It is tempting to dimiss these findings as age specific. However, there is no difference between the mean age of youths working and those in school.

5. The choice is either no money or illegal money.

REFERENCES

AKERS, R. L. (1977) Deviant Behavior: A Social Learning Approach. Belmont, CA: Wadsworth.

ALFARO, J. (1978) Child Abuse and Subsequent Delinquent Behavior. New York: Select Committee on Child Abuse.

BAKER, B. O. and T. R. SARBIN (1956) "Differential mediation of social adjustment." Sociometry 19: 69-83.

CLOWARD, R. A. and L. E. OHLIN (1960) Delinquency and Opportunity. New York: Free Press.

CONGER, R. D. (1980) "Juvenile delinquency: behavior restraint or behavior facilitation?" in T. Hirschi and M. Gottfredson (eds.) Understanding Crime. Beverly Hills, CA: Sage.

DEROGATIS, L., R. LIPMAN, and L. COVI (1973) "The SCL-90: an outpatient psychiatric rating scale." Pharmacology Bulletin, 9: 13-28.

EARLS, F. (1979) "Social reconstruction of adolescence: toward an explanation for increasing rates of urban violence in youth," in H. M. Rose (ed.) Lethal Aspects of Urban Violence. Lexington, MA: D. C. Heath.

ELLIOTT, D. S. and H. VOSS (1974) Delinqunecy and Dropout. Lexington, MA: D. C. Heath.

ELLIOTT, D. S., S. AGETON, and R. CANTER (1979) "An integrated perspective on delinquent behavior." Journal of Research in Crime and Delinquency 16, 1.

ELLIOTT, D. S., B. KNOWLES, and R. CANTER (1981) "The epidemiology of delinquent behavior and drug use amoung American adolescents, 1976-1978." Boulder, CO: Behavioral Research Institute.

FAGAN, J. A., D. K. STEWART, and K. V. HANSEN (1982) "Violent men or violent husbands? Background factors and situational correlated of spousal violence," in J. Hotaling, J. M. Straus, R. Gelles, and D. Finkelhor (eds.) The Dark Side of Families, Beverly Hills, CA: Sage.

FAGAN, J., V. LEWIS, S. WEXLER, and D. STEWART (1981) National Family Violence Evaluation: Second Interim Report. San Francisco: URSA Institute.

GLASER, D. (1973) "The state of the art of criminal justice evaluation." Keynote speech at the Second Annual Meeting of the Association for Criminal Justice Research, Nov.

GOLD, M. and D. J. REIMER (1975) "Changing patterns of delinquency behavior among Americans 13 through 16 years old.: 1967-1972." Crime and Delinquency 7, 4.

GOTTFREDSON, M. D. (1979) "Treatment destruction techniques." Journal of Research in Crime and Delinquency 16, 1: 39-54.

HAMPARIAN, D. M. (1982) Youth In Adult Courts: Between Two Worlds. Columbus, OH: Academy for Contemporary Problems.

—— R. SCHUSTER, S. DINITZ, and J. P. CONRAD (1978) The Violent Few: A Study of Dangerous Juvenile Offenders. Lexington, MA: D. C. Heath.

HARTSTONE, E., M. JANG, and D. STEWART (1982) "Delinquent careers of the chronically violent juvenile." Paper presented at the annual meeting of the American Society of Criminologists, Toronto.

HASKELL M. R. and L. YABLONSKY (1978) Juvenile Delinquency. Chicago: Rand McNally.

HAWKINS, J. D. and J. G. WEIS (1980) The Social Development Model: An Integrated Approach to Delinquency Prevention. Seattle: Center for Law and Justice, University of Washington.

HIRSCHI, T. (1969) Causes of Delinquency. Berkeley: University of California Press.

LERMAN, P. (1975) Community Treatment and Scoical Control: A Critical Analysis of Juvenile Correctional Policy. Chicago: University of Chicago Press.

McDERMOTT, J. and M. HINDELANG (1981) Analysis of National Crime Victimization Survey Data to Study Serious Delinquent Behavior. Albany, NY: Criminal Justice Research Center.

MILLER, A. and L. OHLIN (1980) Decision-Making About Secure Care for Juveniles. Cambridge: Harvard University, Center for Criminal Justice.

MILLER, W. B. (1976) Violence by Young Gangs and Youth Groups as a Crime Problem in Major American Cities: Interim Report. Washington, DC: Government Printing Office.

—————— (1976) Violence by Youth Gangs and Youth Groups in Major American Cities: Final Report. Cambridge: Harvard University Law School.

MONAHAN, J. (1980) Predicting Violent Behavior: An Assessment of Clinical Techniques. Beverly Hills, CA: Sage.

—————— (1977) "The prediction of violent behavior in juveniles, " in J. Hudson and P. Mack (eds.) The Serious Juvenile Offender: Proceedings of a Symposium. Washington, DC: Office of Juvenile Justice and Delinquency Prevention.

ROBISON, J. and G. SMITH (1971) "The effectiveness of correctional programs." Crime and Delinquency 17, 1.

ROJECK, D. and M. ERICKSON (1982) "Delinquent careers: A test of the career escalation model." Criminology 20,1.

SADOFF, R. L. (1978) "Violence in juveniles" in R. L. Sadoff (ed.) Violence and Responsibility. Flushing, NY: Spectrum Publications.

SCHUR, E. (1973) Radical Non-Intervention: Rethinking the Delinquency Problem. Englewood Cliffs, NJ: Prentice-Hall.

SECHREST, L. and R. REDNER (1978) "Strength and integrity of treatments in evaluation studies," in How Well Does It Work? Review of Criminal Justice Evaluation. Washington, DC: National Institute of Law Enforcement and Criminal Justice.

SHANNON, L. (1981) "Protecting adult careers from juvenile careers." Unpublished paper, Iowa Urban Community Research Center, Universtiy of Iowa.

SORRELS, J. (1980) "What can be done about juvenile homicide?" Crime and Delinquency (April): 152-61.

—————— (1977) "Kids who kill." Crime and Delinquency 23, 3: 312-20.

STRASBURG, P. (1978) Violent Delinquents: A Report to the Ford Foundation from the Vera Institute of Justice. New York: Monarch.

SUBLETT, S. (1977) "An Illinois perspective on the problem of the serious juvenile offender "The Serious Juvenile Offender. Washington, DC: Office of Juvenile Justice and Delinquecy Prevention.

THORNBERRY, T. P. and M. FARNSWORTH (1981) "Social correlated of criminal involvement: further evidence on the relationship between social status and criminal behavior." Presented at the annual meeting of the American Society of Criminology, Washington, D.C.

VACHSS, A. H. and Y. BAKAL (1979) Life-Style Violent Juvenile—The Secure Treatment Approach. Lexington, MA: D. C. Heath

WEIS, J. and J. SEDERSTROM (1981) The Prevention of Serious Delinquency: What to Do? Seattle: University of Washington, Center for Law and Justice.

WOLFGANG, M. E. (1978). "Sociology of agression: crime and violence." Australian Journal of Forensic Sciences 11, 1: 3-32.

——————, R. FIGLIO, and T. SELLIN (1972) Delinquency in a Birth Cohort. Chicago: University of of Chicago Press.

7

Ronald A. Feldman

Timothy E. Caplinger
Washington University
St. Louis, Missouri

THE ST. LOUIS EXPERIMENT
Treatment of Antisocial Youths in Prosocial Peer Groups

Little documentation is needed to support the contention that juvenile delinquency imposes extraordinary costs on American society. The rate of arrests for persons under 18 years appears to be declining vis-à-vis other age groups. Yet, the total numbers of arrested youths is on the rise. According to the Statistical Abstracts of the United States (U. S. Bureau of the Census, 1979: 185), for instance, 27.2% of persons arrested in 1974 were under 18 years of age. This figure declined to 23.3% in 1978. Nevertheless, the 1974 figure represents a total of 1,683,000 youths while the one for 1978 represents 2,279,000 youths. From virtually any perspective, the numbers of young offenders in America are extraordinarily high and the financial and social burdens they impose on society are enormous. For example, Vereb and Finnegan (1978: 11) report that 20.0 youths per 1000, aged 10 through 17 years, were formally adjudicated by juvenile courts in 1958, while 39.9 per 1000 were handled in 1975. During this period, the number of young males who appeared before juvenile courts tripled

AUTHORS' NOTE: This study was supported by means of Research Grant MH-18813 from the Center for Studies of Crime and Delinquency, National Institute of Mental Health.

from 383,000 to 1,001,685. From a purely fiscal perspective, Higgins (1977) estimates that the long-term costs incurred by early offenders (that is, those whose first offense is a minor or index crime) are $934 million in California alone.

To reduce such burdens for American society, policymakers and administrators must begin to identify the processes that underlie the development of delinquent careers and, in turn, to devise effective programs of primary, secondary, or tertiary prevention. Only in recent years, however, have there been sufficent advances in research methodology for investigators to trace the sequential development of delinquent careers in a reliable fashion. Major impetus in this regard was provided by the landmark study of delinquency in a birth cohort by Wolfgang et al. (1972). Among other things, this research highlighted the advisability of gearing delinquency prevention and rehabilitation programs toward youths who are in preadolescence or early adolescence. The investigators' data revealed that the curve for first offenses tends to peak at age 13. Moreover, boys who committed a delinquent act at age 13 were responsible for 1,406 of the 10,214 offenses reported for their cohort. Close to 87% of the delinquent acts recorded by Wolfgang and his colleagues scored below 300 on an index of seriousness. For the most part, then, their subjects engaged in relatively minor forms of delinquency, such as petty theft, during the early stages of a delinquent career. Almost one-third of the delinquencies involved apprehensions for curfew violations, truancy, trespassing, and similar activities. Recent longitudinal research suggests that offenses such as these are relatively good predictors of more serous deliquency at later ages (see, for example, Farrington, 1977, 1979; Olson, 1978; Robins and Wish, 1977).

In conjunction with recent methodological advances, Patterson (1982) has demonstrated that childhood noncompliance to parents is associated with ever-increasing risks for more serious varieties of antisocial behavior. Each phase in the developmental process becomes more problematic than the preceding ones. For example, frequent fights with one's siblings are succeeded in turn by teasing, temper tantrums, and more serious antisocial acts. Lying to one's parents, too, is associated subsequently with a greater likelihood of uncontrolled "running around" with antisocial peers. This, in turn, progresses to higher risk status for stealing and, then, for setting fires. Comparable methodologies have been introduced by Farrington (1979) in order to examine the longitudinal development of delinquent careers.

For both research and intervention, the implications of such studies are manifold. Since serious behavioral problems tend to be preceded by less serious misbehaviors, it is obvious that well-targeted efforts at secondary prevention must begin at early stages of deviant career development. However, serious behavioral problems, such as homicide and assault, tend to occur at low base rates while less serious ones occur at higher base rates. Hence, it is advisable from both a clinical and a research perspective to implement and evaluate interventions that are directed primarily toward the latter types of problems rather than the former. The developmental chronology of differential base rates points to the need for initiating intervention programs during the early states of delinquent careers. Equally germane, if intervention programs are to take place at early developmental stages, they must be conducted in the open community rather than in closed correctional institutions. This is due both to the tender age of early offenders and the relatively mild nature of their misbehavior at the beginning stages of a delinquent career. Unfortunately, efforts to treat youths in open settings have experienced great difficuly in generating initial behavioral changes. Once generated, however, it is plausible to assume that such changes will be stabilized and maintained more readily than those that occur in closed correctional institutions. This suggests that it is imperative to ascertain the particular features of community-based intervention programs that are most likely to prevent nascent delinquents from developing into seasoned criminals.

Community-based treatment programs, according to many observers, are superior to programs that are conducted in closed correctional institutions. Among other things, the latter programs are hindered frequently by manpower deficiencies, overcrowding, exorbitant operating costs, countertherapeutic pressures from delinquent peers, inadequate generalization of behavioral changes to the open community, and adverse labeling and stigmatization that devolve in part from the treatment setting itself. However, the actual results of community-based treatment do not provide clear evidence of their superiority (see Empey and Erickson, 1972; Warren, 1976; Lerman, 1975; Lipton, Martinson, and Wilks, 1975; Wright and Dixon, 1977). At best, some critics argue, the two types of programs achieve relatively similar levels of success and/or failure. Community-based programs are thus favored primarily on the basis of lower costs rather than superiority in generating long-term behavioral changes.

Whether one considers programs in closed or open settings, however, it is especially pertinent to ascertain the particular features of the treatment context that deter client progress and, in turn, that can be modified in order to enhance the effectiveness of intervention. As suggested by Palmer (1975), it is essential to ascertain what works in various circumstances rather than to assume that all programs of a given genre are failures. Similarly, one must ponder why community-based treatment programs have fared little, if at all, better than treatment programs in closed settings.

From our own perspective, treatment programs for antisocial youths typically suffer from two basic deficiencies regardless of whether they take place in closed institutions or relatively open facilities. In both settings subjects are treated among peers who have been identified as antisocial. As a result, the treatment context—even if in the open community—provides a surfeit of deviant role models and peer reinforcements for antisocial or countertherapeutic behavior (see, for example, Buehler et al., 1966). Moreover, even when treated successfully, subjects who are discharged from such programs are prone to stigmatization or adverse labeling that emanates, at least in part, from their association with a "correctional," "mental health," or "treatment" facility. Following interviews with 36 institutionalized male youths, for example, Newton and Sheldon (1975) showed that the more one's status of "deviant" is reinforced by others, the more one tends to view oneself as deviant and to behave accordingly. Farrington (1977) likewise demonstrated that adverse public labeling strengthens the probabililty of increased deviance. His data suggest that the effects of adverse labeling are cumulative and that youths who are first labeled before the age of 14 suffer more persistent effects than those who are so labeled at a later age. Severance and Gasstrom (1977) demonstrated, furthermore, that the imputation of a negative label reduces the likelihood that a youngster will be properly credited for his behavior when he does, in fact, conduct himself in a prosocial manner.

How, then, can one avert such formidable barriers to the effective treatment of antisocial youths? Optimally, it would seem advisable to establish treatment programs for antisocial youths in community-based settings that are minimally stigmatizing, if at all, and to engage large numbers of prosocial—rather than antisocial—peers in the treatment process. But simple as the solution may be in theory, practical reasons underlie the fact that such programs are virtually nonexistent in juvenile corrections. Foremost is the suspicion—if not the outright fear—that the prosocial participants in such programs are likely to develop deviant behavioral patterns as a result of exposure to antisocial or delinquent peers. This concern cannot be vitiated in the absence of rigorous empirical evidence to the contrary.

Accordingly, the present research examines three basic questions. First, can effective group treatment programs for antisocial youths be provided in a "traditional" community center that is not identified publicly as a "correctional" or "mental health" facility? Second, can behavioral changes on the part of antisocial youths be generated more readily when they are treated among prosocial peers rather than among antisocial peers? And, third, does participation in integrated group treatment programs bring about adverse behavioral changes among prosocial youths?

METHOD

Known locally as the Group Integration Project and nationally as the St. Louis Experiment (Center for Studies of Crime and Delinquency, 1974), the program described here was established at the Jewish Community Centers Association (JCCA), St. Louis, Missouri. Begun in the early 1970s, the final results of the program have been reported thus far only in partial and preliminary fashion (see, for example, Feldman and Caplinger, 1977; Gingerich et al., 1977; Feldman et al., 1975). Therefore, the present discussion attempts to summarize the main effects of the program on the 701 youngsters who participated in it. Elsewhere, a more detailed discussion examines the theoretical rationales, research methods, group influence processes, and interactive relationships that occurred during the course of the St. Louis Experiment (Feldman et al., 1983).

Subjects

Only two categories of subjects participated in the research: nonreferred subjects and referred subjects. Nonreferred subjects were boys between 7 and 15 years of age who were regularly enrolled members at the JCCA. Referred subjects were males between the ages of 7 and 15 who were referred to the program by the professional staff of juvenile courts, special schools, mental health facilities, and residential treatment centers. Referral was facilitated by means of a referral checklist. The latter required a referral agent to estimate the number of times during the preceding seven days that a referred youth engaged in a variety of criterion behaviors deemed to hurt, disrupt, or annoy others. These included antisocial motor behaviors, physical contacts, verbalizations, object interference, and distracting others. To qualify for an enrollment interview it was necessary for the referral agent to report that a youth engaged in at least 21 antisocial behaviors per week. However, referral agents never were told about this quantitative criterion for enrollment. When a referred youth scored above the criterion, he and his parents were invited to an intake interview. The parents then completed a similar checklist. To be admitted to the St. Louis Experiment, the boy's parents had to confirm independently that he engaged in 21 or more antisocial acts per week. The product-moment correlation for scores on the referral agent and parent checklist was .51 (p < .001), thus indicating a modest degree of agreement.

The mean age of referred subjects was 11.2 years. While 64.8% were white, 34.3% were black and 0.9% were classified as "other." As inferred from data regarding their mothers' religion, 66.3% of the referred boys were Protestant, 23.4% were Catholic, 5.6% were Jewish, and 4.8% were "other." Using Census Bureau occupational categories (Reiss et al., 1961), 12.5% of the referred boys' fathers were regarded as professional, 13.0% as managerial, 32.3% as skilled, 33.2% as unskilled, 3.8% as unemployed, and 5.3% as "other." By contrast, the parents of the nonreferred boys were predominantly white, Jewish, and from higher occupational brackets.

Research Design

The St. Louis Experiment employed a 3 x 3 x 2 factorial design (see Table 7.1). Three major sets of variables were studied: mode of group composition (referred groups vs. nonreferred groups vs. mixed, or integrated, groups), group treatment method (social learning method vs. traditional group work vs. minimal treatment), and extent of group leader's prior experience (experienced vs. inexperienced). All groups were stratified by age. The referred groups (N = 25) consisted of 237 referred youths. Nonreferred groups (N = 13) consisted of 174 nonreferred youths. Mixed groups (N = 22) consisted of 264 nonreferred youths plus one or two referred youths (N = 26) who had been assigned to them on a random basis. All told, this design yielded four discrete samples of subjects: referred youths in unmixed groups, referred youths in mixed groups, nonreferred youths in mixed groups and nonreferred youths in unmixed groups. To facilitate the analyses that appear below these subjects will be denoted, respectively, as RU-boys, RM-boys, NM-boys, and NU-boys.

Elsewhere, the group treatment methods implemented during the St. Louis Experiment are described in substantial detail (Feldman and Wodarski, 1975). In brief, however, the social learning method primarily entails the use of group-level behavior modification. For ease of description the social learning method will be referred to hereafter as the behavioral method. The traditional group work method, in contrast, entails the application of interventions that are based on social psychological and social group work principles. No training or systematic interventions were entailed on the part of minimal-method group leaders. Instead, the practitioners of this method were encouraged to interact with group members in a natural and spontaneous fashion. Only after the conclusion of an eight-week baseline period were the respective methods taught to the group leaders.

Experienced group leaders were students at a graduate school of social work (either Washington University in St. Louis or St. Louis University) while the inexperienced leaders were untrained undergraduate students. Assignment of virtually all group leaders and treatment methods was made on a random basis. Within the aforementioned framework, two cohorts of subjects participated primarily in a variety of recreational and leisure-time activities. Their groups met approximately once per week at the JCCA throughout the school year and for an average of 22.2 meetings.

Measures

Throughout the research, the subjects' proportionate behavioral profiles were systematically examined. As Achenbach (1978: 25) notes, much research focuses exclusively on pathological behavior and therefore excludes positive adaptive behavior. To countervail this tendency, most inventories and observa-

TABLE 7.1 Research Design Implemented for the St. Louis Experiment Total N = 701 Subjects and 50 Groups

	Leader Training						
	Experienced Leaders			Inexperienced Leaders			
	Treatment Method			Treatment Method			
Group Composition	Behavioral Method	Traditional Method	Minimal Method	Behavioral Method	Traditional Method	Minimal Method	Total
Referred	Ss = 61 Gs = 6	Ss = 41 Gs = 4	Ss = 37 Gs = 4	Ss = 34 Gs = 4	Ss = 25 Gs = 3	Ss = 39 Gs = 4	Ss = 237 Gs = 25
Mixed	Ss = 55 Gs = 4 (5)	Ss = 50 Gs = 4 (5)	Ss = 44 Gs = 3 (4)	Ss = 30 Gs = 4 (4)	Ss = 61 Gs = 4 (4)	Ss = 50 Gs = 3 (4)	Ss = 290 Gs = 22 (26)
Non-Referred	Ss = 38 Gs = 3	Ss = 22 Gs = 2	Ss = 14 Gs = 1	Ss = 40 Gs = 3	Ss = 30 Gs = 2	Ss = 30 Gs = 2	Ss = 174 Gs = 13
	Ss = 154 Gs = 13	Ss = 113 Gs = 10	Ss = 95 Gs = 9	Ss = 104 Gs = 10	Ss = 116 Gs = 9	Ss = 119 Gs = 9	Ss = 701 Gs = 60

Key:

Ss = Number of subjects per cell.
Gs = Number of groups per cell.
( ) = Number of referred subjects assigned to each mixed group category.

tional systems for the St. Louis Experiment examined three types of behavior. *Prosocial behavior* was defined operationally as any action by a group member that was directed toward completion of a peer group's tasks or activities. *Antisocial behavior* was defined as any action that disrupts, hurts, or annoys other members, or that otherwise prevents them from participating in the group's tasks or activities. *Nonsocial behavior* was defined as any action that is not directed toward completion of a group's tasks or activities but that does not interfere with another youth's participation in the group's tasks or activities. By analyzing these particular behaviors it was possible to calculate each subject's proportionate behavioral profile at any particular juncture of the program. Accordingly, delinquent behavior was not treated merely as a dichotomous attribute, or as something that one either is or is not (see Short, 1960; Empey 1969).

At pretest and posttest, behavioral checklists were completed by the referral agents, parents, group leaders, and the youths themselves. These checklists asked the respondents to estimate the frequency with which a given youth exhibited various types of prosocial, nonsocial, and antisocial behavior during a seven-day period. In addition, throughout the entire project trained nonpartici-pant observers employed a 10-second summated partition sampling system that classified each subject's actual behavior into similar prosocial, nonsocial, and antisocial categories. All observations for each subject were tabulated after each group meeting. As a result, it was possible to report the proportion of each subject's behavior that was either prosocial, nonsocial, or antisocial during a given group meeting. To meet customary requirements for the statistical analy-sis of percentage and proportionate data, an arc sine transformation was performed for all of the proportionate behavioral scores (Winer, 1971: 400). Furthermore, to facilitate the delineation of longitudinal trends, the data for all sessions were collapsed into four successive periods of approximately eight weeks each: baseline, T1, T2, and T3. Nonparticipant observers were evaluated every two weeks by comparing their ratings of different videotapes of group interaction with those of an "expert judge." They were allowed to work only if their reliability was consistently at a level of .90 or above. Across all sessions, the mean reliability ratio for observers was 92.2. A ratio of interobserver agreement, interval by interval, was derived from the following formula:

$$\text{Ratio of interobserver agreement} = \frac{\text{N of agreements}}{\text{N of agreements} + \text{N of disagreements}}$$

Nonparticipant observers and group leaders also provided data that enabled determination of each subject's extent of normative, functional, and interper-sonal integration into his respective peer group. Specifically, an individual's normative integration into a group refers to the extent to which he adheres to basic norms that are shared by his peers. Functional integration refers to the extent to which he contributes effectively to the attainment of key group goals such as goal attainment, pattern maintenance, and external relations. Interpersonal integration reflects the extent to which he likes others in the group *and* is liked by them. The theoretical rationales and mathematical procedures for calculating subjects' scores on each of these dimensions are described elsewhere (see Feldman, 1968, 1969, 1972, 1973; Feldman et al., 1983). Pretest and posttest responses to the Manifest Aggression Subscale of the Jesness Inventory (1972) also were obtained from the subjects.

Besides conventional univariate analyses, multivariate analyses of the data were performed by means of composite measures that distinguished between the referred and nonreferred samples. Typically, the composite measures combined information from each of the five basic self-report instruments that were employed during the research (mean manifest aggression scores, absolute frequencies of antisocial behavior, and proportionate mean incidences of antisocial, nonsocial, and prosocial behavior). Differences between the two samples were ascertained by means of standardized discriminant analyses (Kaplan and Litrownik, 1977; Bock, 1975). As seen in the figures that follow, when discriminant scores are averaged for all cases within a particular group, it is possible to obtain group centroids, or means, for the multiple measures that define a discriminant function. Group centroids depict complex multivariate findings in a relatively straightforward fashion. Clustering among centroids denotes great similarities among groups of subjects while various degrees of separation depict the magnitude of differences among them. Centroids are plotted in a direction that denotes the relative presence or absence of problem behavior among the groups of subjects (see Feldman et al., 1983).

To transcend some of the analytical problems that are associated with classical experimental designs, analyses of covariance were employed for the assessment of pretest-posttest changes among the subjects. As Huck and McLean (1975) and Roscoe (1969) note, pretest data are the concomitant variable in the analysis of covariance, thereby partialing out that portion of variance in subjects' posttest scores that can be predicted from pretest scores. The foremost advantage of covariance analysis, as opposed to the simple analysis of gain scores, inheres in the reduction of error variance. In addition, covariance analyses help to reduce errors in interpretation that might be due to regressions to the mean. This is accomplished by subtracting from the raw measures of change (or postscores) a function of the subjects' initial level of performance. Covariance analysis generally improves precision in the assessment of treatment effects (see Lord, 1967). Nonetheless, it is imperative to correct for measurement errors in analyses of covariance that are attributable to the unreliability of subjects' prescores (Cronbach and Furby, 1970). The assessments reported here employ a method for reliability-corrected covariance analyses wherein subjects' "true" prescores are estimated and then utilized to determine pretest-posttest "gains" (Porter, 1967).

End point analyses, dropout analyses, and survivor analyses were employed in order to determine longitudinal variations in the subjects' scores. Specifically, end point analyses are performed by examining each subject's behavioral profile for the *last* time period (that is, T1, T2, or T3) during which he participated in the program. Analyses of end point data are performed by means of a multivariate analysis of covariance in which the subjects' observed baseline behaviors serve as the concomitant variate. Such analyses can be performed either for dropouts (that is, youths who quit the program after the baseline period but before the commencement of T3) or for survivors (that is, subjects who remained in the program for the full year, or throughout T3). In addition, whenever indicated, a posteriori tests for individual comparisons are conducted by means of Hotelling's T^2 statistic (Bock, 1975).

RESULTS

The results of the St. Louis Experiment can be gauged best by summarizing the subjects' pretest behavior and then proceeding to a discussion of the experimental outcomes reported by a variety of different sources (nonparticipant observers, group leaders, the youths, parents, and referral agents).

Pretest Behavior of the Subjects

Several different perspectives of the subjects' behavior are provided by the above-cited measures. Using the behavioral checklist, for example, parents of referred youths estimated at intake that their sons engaged in 26.5 antisocial acts per week, or about 4 per day. About 35% of their sons' behavior was considered antisocial. Referral agents reported even greater incidences of antisocial behavior on the part of such boys. In their judgment, referred boys committed 62.7 antisocial acts per week, representing 59% of their total behavior. The referral agents' estimates were significantly higher than those reported by the boys' parents ($p < .001$). Although completed several months apart, the pretest proportionate estimates from referral agents were correlated moderately with those from the group leaders ($r = .34$, $p < .001$) and with the baseline proportionate data reported by nonparticipant observers ($r = .26$, $p < .01$). Since this was not so for the parents' pretest reports, the respondents' data may have somewhat greater cross-situational reliability for settings such as schools and recreational centers than for the subjects' homes. Group leaders, too, reported significant pretest differences between the proportionate antisocial behavior of referred and nonreferred youths (respectively, M = 35.2% vs. M = 26.7%, $p < .01$).

Behavioral self-reports from the referred and nonreferred youths showed much less pretest variation between the two samples. On a univariate basis, referred youths reported higher proportionate incidences of nonsocial behavior (p < .001) and higher scores on manifest aggression (p < .001) at pretest, but no differences in absolute incidences of antisocial behavior or in proportionate incidences of prosocial or antisocial behavior. At least in part, however, self-reported nonsocial behavior may represent a passive-aggressive form of antisocial activity. Even more important, the two samples of youths differed significantly at pretest on the basis of the multivariate composite measure of self-reported behavior (chi-square (5) = 31.05, p < .001). Also, referred youths reported significantly higher pretest scores on manifest aggression than did the nonreferred youths (p < .001).

Baseline data from the nonparticipant observers are somewhat similar to those reported by the youths. That is, the composite measure revealed significant pretest differences between the referred and nonreferred boys (chi-square (3) = 22.4, p < .001). However, the differences were primarily in terms of the subjects' proportionate nonsocial behavior rather than their antisocial or prosocial behavior. Notably, the nonparticipant observers and the group leaders tended to agree about the youths' pretreatment mean proportionate incidences of antisocial (r = .44, p < .001), nonsocial (r = .25, p < .001), and prosocial (r = .42, p < .001) behavior.

Concurrently, the group leaders and the nonparticipant observers reported that referred youths had significantly lower pretest scores than nonreferred youths with reference to social power and normative, functional, and interpersonal integration (p < .001). This suggests that the nonreferred youths may have been able to exert considerable influence over their groupmates while the referred boys may have been more vulnerable to such influence. At the same time, the nonreferred boys may have been better able to resist undue pressures toward antisocial behavior. The relatively strong norm consensus among nonreferred youths in mixed groups may have been a key determinant of behavior change among the referred boys in their groups. A composite measure (consisting of combined scores for social power, normative integration, functional integration, and interpersonal integration) showed particularly strong pretreatment differences between the two samples of youths, whether reported by group leaders (chi-square (4) = 39.2, p < .001) or nonparticipant observers (chi-square (4) = 35.0, p < .001). At pretest, the group leaders and nonparticipant observers expressed considerable agreement about the subjects' social power (r = .41, p < .001), normative integration (r = .41, p < .001), functional integration (r = .45, p < .001), and interpersonal integration (r = .51, p < .001).

Behavioral Changes from the Perspective of Nonparticipant Observers

Changes in the subjects' behavior may vary in accord with differences in leader experience, treatment method, and peer group composition. Hence, it is informative to consider the effects of these variables separately.

Leader experience. Initial analyses of the end point data for behavioral changes among the subjects are summarized in Table 7.2. These data, which were obtained by the trained nonparticipant observers, reveal significant posttest behavioral differences between youths who were treated either by experienced or inexperienced group leaders. As depicted in Figure 7.1, boys who were treated by experienced leaders benefited considerably more from the program than did comparable boys who were treated by inexperienced leaders (T^2 = 48.4, p < .001). The group centroids represent a composite of the multiple changes that were observed in the subjects' proportionate mean incidences of antisocial, nonsocial, and prosocial behavior. In specific terms, the data reveal that E-boys (that is, boys in groups with experienced leaders) displayed marked reductions in proportionate antisocial (M = –3.1%, p < .001) and nonsocial (M = –1.9%, p < .001) behavior. By the end of treatment, 96.7% of the E-boys' observed behavior was prosocial. This represents a substantial upturn in prosocial behavior (M = +5.0%, p < .001) from their mean pretreatment incidence. At the end of treatment, only 2.4% of the E-boys' behavior was antisocial.

In marked contrast, 6.9% of the I-boys' behavior was antisocial at end point. This represents nearly three times the incidence for E-boys. The I-boys exhibited significantly higher posttreatment incidences of antisocial behavior (M = +1.4%, p < .001). It is equally useful to note that 83.2% of the E-boys exhibited prosocial gains during the program while only 54.7% of the I-boys did so. This difference between the two samples is statistically significant (chi-square (1) = 42.0, p < .001). Above and beyond the youths' baseline behavior, however, only 9.6% of the variance in treatment outcomes was explained by the differential effectiveness of experienced and inexperienced leaders (r_{cc} = .31, p < .001). Additional factors, therefore, must account for the observed changes in the youths' behavior.

When the comparable data for continuers and discontinuers are examined (see Figure 7.2), the foregoing trends appear to be strengthened rather than weakened. For instance, when assigned to experienced leaders, even early discontinuers (N = 65) exhibited a notable reduction in antisocial behavior (M = –2.6%, p < .004). As seen in Figure 7.2, their outcomes are not significantly different from the ones displayed by EC-boys (that is, boys who were treated by experienced leaders and who continued for the entire program). For ED-boys, then, early discontinuance does not necessarily represent an instance of treatment failure. Longitudinal analyses show, moreover, that the experienced leaders were able to bring about marked declines in the subjects' antisocial behavior quite rapidly (that is, during T1) and to sustain them over time. By way of comparison, boys who were treated by inexperienced leaders exhibited negative behavioral outcomes, especially when they quit the program at an early point.

Treatment method. Method of treatment, in contrast with the findings for leader experience, seems to exert little or no impact on behavior change. The

TABLE 7.2 Multivariate Analyses of Covariance for Observed Changes in Behavior, End Point Data (N = 452)

Source	df	SSCP[a]			Standardized Discriminant Coefficients	Multivariate F
		Percentage Antisocial	Percentage Nonsocial	Percentage Prosocial		
Leaders	1	2.62			-.88	14.86***
		1.51	.87		-.48	
		5.25	3.03	10.52	.16	
Methods	2	.48			-.85	2.22*
		.31	.27		-.53	
		1.02	.82	6.94	.18	
Groups	2	.66			1.00	2.07*
		-.13	.11		-.43	
		1.45	.02	4.26	-.04	
Leaders × Methods	2	.26			-.59	1.90
		.02	.00		.19	
		.61	-.06	9.34	1.19	
Leaders × Groups	2	1.55			1.10	4.15***
		-.12	.14		-.27	
		2.25	.06	3.70	-.24	
Methods × Groups	4	.64			.78	3.28***
		-.25	.86		-.66	
		.22	2.88	15.68	-.74	
Leaders × Methods × Groups	4	1.02			1.09	1.84*
		.09	.28		-.09	
		1.96	.46	7.53	-.16	
Error	431	32.68				
		4.65	23.39			
		75.85	23.24	622.01		

*p < .05
***p < .001
a. Sum of squares and cross products.

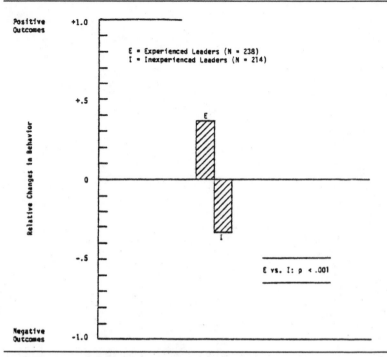

Figure 7.1   Group Controls for the Effects of Leader Experience on Observed Changes in Behavior: End Point Data

behavioral method fostered significantly better outcomes than traditional group work (p < .001). Still, it fared no better than the minimal method (p < .79). In addition, an assessment of interaction effects suggests that experienced leaders achieved relatively positive outcomes regardless of which treatment method they applied. Inexperienced leaders, on the other hand, had relatively negative outcomes, especially when they applied traditional group work.

Group composition. Unlike some of the analyses that appear below, the observational data suggest a rather weak relationship between group composition and treatment outcomes (see figure 7.3). Nonetheless, most of the trends are in the expected direction. For example, while the observed antisocial behavior of RU-boys did not decline over time (M = +0.3%, p < .70), it dropped significantly among RM-boys (M = –2.2%, p < .01). At end point, 5.7% of the observed behavior of RU-boys was antisocial while only 3.2% of the behavior of RM-boys was antisocial. Similarly, 91.3% of the RM-boys experienced a discernible decline in antisocial behavior while only 50.9% of the RU-boys did so. In comparison, 72.2% of the NM-boys and 65.5% of the NU-boys experienced a decline in antisocial behavior (chi-square (3) = 24.6, p

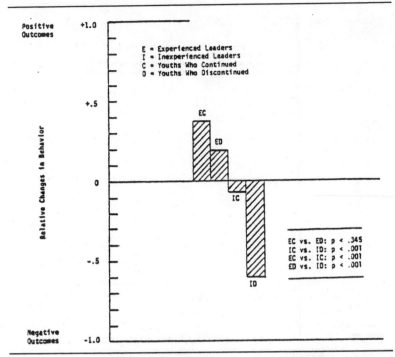

E = Experienced Leaders
I = Inexperienced Leaders
C = Youths Who Continued
D = Youths Who Discontinued

EC vs. ED: p < .345
IC vs. ID: p < .001
EC vs. IC: p < .001
ED vs. ID: p < .001

Figure 7.2   Group Controls for the Effects of Leader Experience on Observed Changes in Behavior: Comparison of Youths Who Continued or Discontinued Treatment, Using End Point Data

< .001). By end point, the behavioral patterns of RM-boys differed very little from the nonreferred members of their groups (p < .26). Conversely, the end point behavior of RU-boys differed greatly from NU-boys (p < .03). It is noteworthy, however, that no significant differences were found between the end point behavioral profiles of the NM-boys and NU-boys ($T^2 = 2.2$, p < .34), even though the former were exposed to one or two antisocial youths for prolonged periods.

Once discontinuance is examined, the above trends become even more definitive. When placed in mixed groups, for example, the referred youths benefited from treatment regardless of whether they continued for the full duration (RMC-boys) or discontinued at an early point (RMD-boys). Antisocial behavior constituted only 2.5% of the end point behavioral profile of RMD-boys while it constituted 10.4% for RUD-boys (referred boys in unmixed groups who discontinued from treatment). RMD-boys, therefore, tended to discontinue from treatment primarily after they had established relatively stable patterns of prosocial behavior. In such cases, early discontinu-

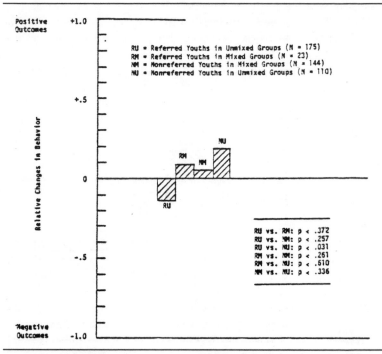

Figure 7.3   Group Controls for the Effects of Group Composition on Observed
Changes in Behavior: End Point Data

ance cannot be regarded as an instance of treatment failure. Interestingly, the
data suggest that the referred boys in unmixed groups achieved behavioral
gains only after the more antisocial members of their treatment group had
departed. Discontinuance of the latter members, in effect, created a treatment
group with behavioral characteristics that were somewhat akin to those of the
mixed, or integrated, groups. The small sizes of the RUD (N = 47) and RMD
(N = 13) subsamples militate against statistically significant trends. Nevertheless, the observational data clearly suggest that referred boys fared better in
integrated groups than in groups comprised solely of referred peers ($T^2 = 5.1$, p
< .09).

Interactions between leader experience and group composition again reveal
that experienced leaders fare better than inexperienced ones in all instances (see
Figure 7.4). But for the first time, the data raise the prospect that nonreferred
boys in mixed groups may not fare as well as nonreferred peers who remain
unexposed to antisocial youths. Even though ENM-boys displayed a significant
decline in antisocial (M = –2.1%, p < .05) and nonsocial (M = –2.0%, p < .001)
behavior and a significant increase in prosocial behavior (M = +4.1%, p < .001),

their gains were not as large as the ones for ENU-boys. Yet, as anticipated, the ERM-boys fared significantly better than IRM-boys ($T^2 = 9.8$, $p < .02$). This finding further supports the likelihood that professional training can help leaders to maximize the therapeutic potential of integrated groups.

The formidable strengths of integrated groups are demonstrated even further when one considers that IRM-boys achieved significant gains in prosocial behavior ($M = +2.7\%$, $p < .02$) even though they were treated by leaders who had no prior training or experience. Such boys also exhibited significant declines in antisocial ($M = -1.7\%$, $p < .05$) and nonsocial ($M = -1.0\%$, $p < .01$) behavior. While they did not benefit to the same extent as ERM-boys, they improved markedly nevertheless. Evidently, then, the beneficial features of integrated groups may compensate for the treatment deficiencies of inexperienced leaders. This supposition is supported by the finding that referred youths fared very poorly when treated in unmixed groups that were led by inexperienced leaders. At end point 9.1% of the behavior of IRU-boys was antisocial, representing a significant increase from baseline ($M = +3.6\%$, $p < .01$). The combination of experienced leaders and mixed peer groups seems to surpass the separate treatment contributions of either variable alone. Three-way interactive analyses demonstrated, further, that the most counterproductive treatment strategy occurred when inexperienced leaders sought to apply traditional group work in unmixed groups of referred youths. This particular combination of variables alone accounts for the three-way interaction that appears in Table 7.2.

Behavioral Changes from the Perspective of Youths and Group Leaders

The respondents who participated most actively in the intervention program were the youths and their group leaders. They were asked to complete behavioral checklists that permitted both absolute and proportionate determinations of the youths' antisocial behavior. Whereas the nonparticipant observers collected time-sampling data on a continuous basis, the youths and group leaders provided self-report data at only two junctures of the program, namely, at the end of the eight-week baseline period and at the conclusion of treatment.

Leader experience. Like the observational data, the pertinent self-report data indicate that youths with experienced leaders had relatively positive outcomes while youths with inexperienced leaders had relatively negative outcomes. As indicated in Table 7.3, however, the differences between the two samples are not statistically significant ($F(5,273) = 1.12$, $p < .35$). On an absolute basis, I-boys (that is, boys who were treated by inexperienced leaders) reported a significant increase in antisocial behavior between pretest and posttest ($M = +45.9$, $p < .03$). Still, when examined in proportionate terms both I-boys and E-boys (that is, boys who were treated by experienced leaders) reported slight,

TABLE 7.3 Multivariate Analyses of Covariance for Youth Self-Reported Changes in Behavior (N = 300)

Source	df	SSCP					Standardized Discriminant Coefficients	Multivariate F
		Absolute Antisocial	Manifest Aggression	Percentage Antisocial	Percentage Nonsocial	Percentage Prosocial		
Leaders	1	74,757.49					-.63	1.12
		-339.74	1.54				.30	
		-96.15	.44	.12			.55	
		-15.04	.06	.02	.00		-.08	
		-268.84	1.22	.34	.05	.97	.68	
Methods	2	63,801.01					.46	.97
		-876.97	17.45				-.23	
		122.98	-.57	.47			.21	
		-183.57	3.03	-.25	.57		-.61	
		123.05	-3.61	-.16	-.53	.92	.55	
Groups	2	201,644.42					.55	2.17*
		-1,204.86	32.47				.13	
		-246.36	-5.41	2.18			-.81	
		-312.18	.30	.81	.58		-.46	
		-307.13	3.10	.03	.40	.53	-.16	
Leaders × Methods	2	83,250.45					.35	3.00***
		4,878.22	374.33				.95	
		105.23	1.14	.42			-.15	
		51.21	8.49	-.25	.37		.22	
		110.33	-1.58	.60	-.43	.88	.33	

Source	df																					
Leaders × Groups	2	10,253.27							-.50		1.13
		-592.84	34.28						.47		
		25.40	-1.45	.12					-.21		
		72.51	-4.20	.13	.55				-.82		
		49.64	-2.92	-.08	.52	.98			-.43		
Methods × Groups	4	365,513.24							.59		1.44
		4,060.11	99.98						.38		
		852.30	16.29	3.20					.53		
		-189.72	-2.95	-.89	.44				-.14		
		-280.46	-5.14	-1.67	.88	2.25			.22		
Leaders × Methods × Groups	4	386,013.22							.48		1.63*
		1,702.13	24.02						.19		
		996.61	7.33	3.23					.56		
		-340.72	-3.81	-1.02	1.24				-.47		
		-492.06	2.13	-.68	-.38	2.32			.37		
Error	277	9,223,097.16									
		31,884.12	5,249.80								
		8,128.25	140.75	91.70							
		-3,922.88	35.41	-2.69	34.98						
		-10,454.22	-222.89	-29.16	.70	115.82					

*p < .05
***p < .001

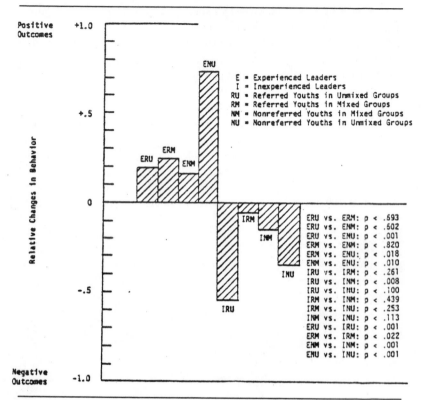

Figure 7.4   Group Controls for the Effects of Leader Experience and Mode of
Group Composition on Observed Changes in Behavior: End Point Data

but insignificant, declines in antisocial behavior. In concert with the findings reported by the nonparticipant observers and group leaders, this suggests the efficacy of analyzing antisocial behavior in terms of its proportionate contribution to a youth's behavioral profile. In addition, this approach takes due cognizance of a related finding: the activity levels of E-boys rose in all areas of comportment (that is, in terms of prosocial, nonsocial, and antisocial behavior).

By comparison, data from group leaders indicate that E-boys benefited far more than I-boys from the program ($T^2 = 10.9$, $p < .01$). According to their leaders, 35.7% of the I-boys' posttest behavioral profile was antisocial, indicating a slight increment in such behavior (M = +2.9%, $p < .13$). At the same time, group leaders reported that 28.3% of the E-boys' behavior was antisocial, representing a significant decline (M = –4.5%, $p < .001$). Furthermore, experienced leaders reported improvements among 60.1% of the boys in their groups while inexperienced leaders reported gains among only 45.0% (chi-square (1) = 6.54, p < .01). These findings, in conjunction with data from the nonparticipant observers, lend further support to the conclusion that leader experience is a key determinant of favorable treatment outcomes on the part of antisocial youths.

Treatment method. Both the youths and their group leaders tended to associate favorable outcomes with traditional group work rather than with the behavioral or minimal methods. However, as seen in Table 7.3, the youth-reported variations are not statistically significant. Similarly, the leader-reported variations are insignificant when individual post hoc analyses are performed by means of Hotelling's T^2. One cannot conclude, then, that the repondents regarded either treatment method as clearly superior to the other or, even, to a "minimal treatment" method.

Group composition. As seen in Figure 7.5, significantly better outcomes were reported by the RM-boys than the RU-boys (T^2 = 14.1, p < .01). Again, therefore, the data suggest the efficacy of treating antisocial youths among peers who have no identifiable behavioral problems. When one also considers the nonreferred youths in mixed groups, the self-report data point to the absence of deleterious treatment outcomes for NM-boys. In their own judgment, the behavioral outcomes for NM-boys did not differ significantly from the ones for NU-boys (p < .20). Indeed, at the posttest NM-boys reported 35% fewer antisocial acts than NU-boys. Pretest-posttest comparisons, moreover, revealed no significant changes in proportionate incidences of antisocial, nonsocial, or prosocial behavior on the part of either the NM-boys or the NU-boys.

The outcomes reported by group leaders were generally consistent with the ones reported by the youths themselves. But even though they reported relatively positive outcomes for RM-boys and negative outcomes for RU-boys, the differences were not statistically significant. Like the youths, the group leaders also reported no adverse behavioral outcomes on the part of NM-boys vis-à-vis NU-boys. In fact, their data indicate a sharp decline in proportionate antisocial behavior among NM-boys (M = –6.9%, p < .001) but virtually no change on the part of NU-boys.

As reported by the youths and group leaders, the interactive relationships among the variables cited earlier are quite complex and therefore are reported in detail elsewhere (Feldman et al., 1983). In general, however, the trends are consistent with the ones reported above. For the most part, the youths and the group leaders reported that the combination of mixed groups and experienced leaders yields better treatment outcomes than any other combination. However, certain of the significant findings that result from multivariate analyses of covariance dissipate when Hotelling's T^2 is used to perform more conservative post hoc analyses of the data.

TABLE 7.4 Multivariate Analyses of Covariance for Leader-Reported Changes in Behavior (N = 322)

Source	df	Absolute Antisocial	Percentage Antisocial	Percentage Nonsocial	Percentage Prosocial	Standardized Discriminant Coefficients	Multivariate F
			SSCP				
Leaders	1	200.01				-.41	6.17***
		25.72	3.31			.87	
		-6.05	-.78	.18		-.29	
		-27.85	-3.58	.84	3.88	-.60	
Methods	2	853.05				.42	3.99***
		42.41	2.15			.40	
		-1.21	-.22	.59		.17	
		51.20	2.24	1.04	5.16	.88	
Groups	2	739.57				.01	2.01*
		25.09	.86			-.26	
		5.54	.20	.07		-.19	
		-40.44	-1.53	-.59	5.07	.91	
Leaders × Methods	2	231.91				-.09	1.70
		-6.84	.21			.25	
		-5.41	.11	.42		.60	
		-9.75	.15	1.01	2.45	.78	
Leaders × Groups	2	424.11				-.12	1.31
		3.19	.06			-.02	
		-11.39	-.11	.33		.54	
		-7.97	-.31	.42	2.07	.79	

Source	df						F
Methods × Groups	4	1,970.19	1.33	.35	2.94	1.08	2.16**
		−15.63	.08	.30		−.91	
		6.71	.83			.11	
		−12.27				−.01	
Leaders × Methods × Groups	4	2,328.37	3.55	.81	4.23	−.69	2.82***
		40.48	.99	−.11		.96	
		14.84	−1.65			.22	
		−14.30				−.51	
Error	300	58,135.21	73.04	34.62	122.65		
		1,053.07	1.83	−.34			
		−10.65	−14.62				
		−761.52					

*$p < .05$
**$p < .01$
***$p < .001$

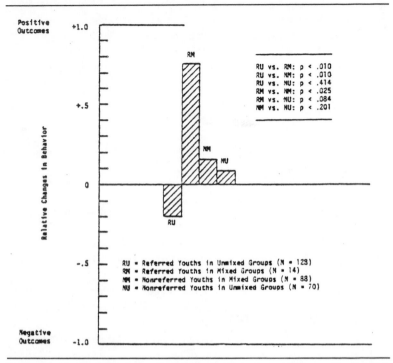

Figure 7.5   Group Controls for the Effects of Group Composition on Youths' Self-Reported Changes in Behavior

Behavioral Changes from the Perspective of Referral Agents and Parents

Owing largely to high rates of mobility and immense variations in their caseloads, it was difficult to obtain complete sets of pretest and posttest data from the referral agents. Indeed, such data were available for only 74 youths. The parents, in contrast, provided complete pretest-posttest data for 140 referred youths. Both the referral agents and the parents reported significant pretest-posttest declines in the antisocial behavior of the referred youths. Moreover, these respondents expressed great consensus about the youths' behavioral gains ($r = .73$, $p < .001$). Unlike other respondents, however, they did not consider experienced group leaders to be particularly more effective than inexperienced ones. Likewise, they reported relatively equal benefits for the referred youths regardless of the types of treatment methods or modes of group composition employed. Though the referral agents and parents reported very positive outcomes from the program, there was little evidence that such findings were attributable to any particular set of independent variables.

A limited follow-up study was conducted one year after completion of the program. Follow-up data from the referral agents were collected for only 27 referred youths while follow-up data from the parents were collected for 54 referred youths. Neither set of respondents reported a significant change in the subjects' antisocial behavior one year after conclusion of the St. Louis Experiment. These limited data suggest that the treatment gains generated during the program were maintained for at least one year after its conclusion.

SUMMARY AND CONCLUSIONS

Contrary to some intervention programs with antisocial youths, a variety of respondents (nonparticipant observers, referral agents, parents, group leaders and youths themselves) tended to concur about the positive treatment outcomes that were achieved by referred antisocial youths who participated in the St. Louis Experiment. Hence, effective group treatment evidently can be provided for antisocial youths in a traditional community center. Such a treatment setting offers several distinct advantages: It is relatively nonstigmatizing and it provides treatment among youths who seldom model antisocial behavior or who reinforce one another for deviant or delinquent behavior.

However, the respondents did not fully agree about the respective contributions of various independent variables to the reported outcomes. Substantial evidence suggests that the referred youths fared best when they were treated in mixed, or integrated, groups and by experienced leaders. Nevertheless, data from some respondents, such as parents and referral agents, do not provide clear support for this conclusion. Related analyses (see Feldman et al., 1983) demonstrate that the mixed and unmixed groups underwent quite different developmental patterns during the St. Louis Experiment. Thus, for example, both group leaders and nonparticipant observers reported the RM-boys became better integrated into their treatment groups by posttest than did RU-boys. Moreover, the RM-boys' longitudinal gains in normative integration and interpersonal integration far exceeded the ones for RU-boys. Gains on these dimensions, as noted by the nonparticipant observers, were associated with reduced incidences of posttest antisocial behavior on the part of RM-boys ($r = .66$, $p < .05$). Furthermore, the RM-boys—unlike the RU-boys—greatly liked their peers and, in turn, were liked by them. Even inexperienced leaders were able to facilitate referred youths' social integration into mixed treatment groups. Experienced leaders, however, were even *more* able to do so.

Concomitantly, a strong association exists between group composition and the particular types of interventions that were applied by the group leaders ($r_{cc} =$

.83, p < .00l). Longitudinal analyses indicate that various interventive activities by the group leaders first modified the behavioral patterns of the treatment group as a whole; thereafter, the modified group altered the behavior of individual members. In mixed groups, for example, the joint effects of the leaders' interventions and program activities accounted for 84% of the total explained variance in youths' behavior change. Related analyses also show that the experienced leaders were more effective than inexperienced ones at promoting peer behavioral changes that subsequently yielded positive outcomes on the part of individual members. In groups that were treated by experienced leaders, nearly 59% of the variance in outcomes among individual members was predicted from antecedent peer behavioral changes. This represents 89% of the total explained variance. Antecedent changes in peer behavior in groups that were treated by inexperienced leaders accounted for only 48% of the variance in individual change, or roughly 67% of the total explained variance. Together, the leaders' interventions and program activities accounted for sizeable proportions of variance in the youths' behavior change, to wit, 84% in mixed groups, 70% in referred groups, and 67% in nonreferred groups. In sum, then, the findings of the St. Louis Experiment point to the efficacy of situating group treatment programs for antisocial youths in relatively nonstigmatizing settings in the open community, such as neighborhood houses, community centers, and recreational agencies. Even further, many—but not all—of the findings point to the particular efficacy of integrating antisocial youths into treatment groups that consist of comparatively prosocial peers who are served by experienced group workers.

REFERENCES

FELDMAN, R. A. and T. E. CAPLINGER (1977) "Social work experience and client behavioral change: a multivariate analysis of process and outcome." Journal of Social Service Research 1: 5-33.
——— and J. S. WODARSKI (1983) The St. Louis Conundrum: The Effective Treatment of Antisocial Youths. Englewood Cliffs, NJ: Prentice-Hall.
FELDMAN, R. A., J. S. WODARSKI, and N. FLAX (1975) "Antisocial children in a summer camp setting: a time-sampling study." Community Mental Health Journal 11: 10-18.
GINGERICH, W. J., R. A. FELDMAN, and J. S. WODARSKI (1977) A behavioral approach toward the labeling of antisocial children." Sociology and Social Research 61: 204-222.
HIGGINS, T. (1977) "The crime costs of California early minor offenders: implications for prevention." Journal of Research in Crime and Delinquency 14: 195-205.
HUCKS, S. W. and R.A. McLEAN (1975) "Using a repeated measures ANOVA to analyze the data from a pretest/posttest design: a potentially confusing task." Psychological Bulletin 82: 511-518.
JESNESS, C. F., W. J. DERISI, P. McCORMICK, and R. F. WEDGE (1972) The Youth Center Research Project. Sacramento: CA: California Youth Authority.
KAPLAN, R. M., and A. D. LITROWNIK (1977) Some statistical methods for the assessment of multiple outcome criteria in behavioral research. Behavior Therapy 8: 383-392.

LIPTON, D., R. MARTINSON, and J. WILKS (1975) The Effectiveness of Correctional Treatment: A Survey of Treatment. New York: Praeger.

LORD, F. M. (1967) "Elementary models for measuring change," in C. W. Harris (ed.) Problems in Measuring Change. Madison: University of Wisconsin Press.

NEWTON, C. and R. G. SHELDON (1975) The delinquent label and its effects on future behavior: an empirical test of Lemert's levels of deviance." International Journal of Criminology and Penology 3: 229-241.

OLSON, M. R. (1978) "Predicting seriousness of official police contact careers: an exploratory analysis." University of Iowa, Iowa Urban Community Research Center. (unpublished)

PALMER, T. (1975) "Martinson revisited." Journal of Research in Crime and Delinquency, 12: 133-152.

PATTERSON, G. R. (1982) Coercive Family Processes. Eugene OR: Castalia Publishing.

PORTER, A. C. (1967) "The effects of using fallible variables in the analysis of covariance." Doctoral dissertation, University of Wisconsin.

REISS, A.J., Jr., O. D. DUNCAN, P. HATT, and G. NORTH (1961) Occupations and Social Status. New York: Free Press.

ROBINS, L. N. and E. WISH (1977) Development of childhood deviance: a study of 223 urban black men from birth to 18," in M. F. McMillan and S. Henao (eds.) Child Psychiatry: Treatment and Research. New York: Brunner/Mazel.

ROSCOE, J. T. (1969) Fundamental Research Statistics for the Behavioral Sciences. New York: Holt, Rinehart & Winston.

SEVERANCE, L. J. and L. L. GASSTROM (1977) "Effects of the label 'mentally retarded' on causal explanations for success and failure outcomes." American Journal of Mental Deficiency 81: 547-555.

United States Bureau of the Census (1979) Statistical Abstracts, 1979. Washington, D C: Government Printing Office.

WARREN, M. Q. (1976) "Intervention with juvenile delinquents," in M. K. Rosenheim (ed.) Pursuing Justice for the Child. Chicago: University of Chicago Press.

WINER, B. J. (1971) Statistical Principles in Experimental Design. New York: McGraw-Hill.

WOLFGANG, M. E., R. M. FIGLIO, and T. SELLIN (1972) Delinquency in a Birth Cohort. Chicago: University of Chicago Press.

WRIGHT, W. E. and M. C. DIXON (1977) "Community prevention and treatment of juvenile delinquency: a review of evaluation studies." Journal of Research in Crime and Delinquency 14: 35-67.

Cheryl L. Maxson

Malcolm W. Klein
University of Southern California

8

GANGS
Why We Couldn't Stay Away

In the summer of 1981, the director of a major gang violence reduction program presented us with the opportunity to become involved with this new program. Despite the fact that one of us had sworn off gang research after suffering burn out from several years of gang intervention design and evaluation in the 1960s, we decided to pursue the opportunity; we just couldn't resist! Various features of the program and the environment in which it was implemented caught our interest, and it is these features we address in this context.

In response to this opportunity, we have collected data from two sources. First, the gang program has afforded an avenue to gather information on the current status of gang structure and membership. These data will be utilized to update the information collected in the 1960s (Klein, 1971). In addition, we are interested in the official definition of incidents as "gang related." The emphasis on definitional and recording issues as they relate to claims of changes in gang activity levels has led us to extensive coding of police investigator files on gang and comparable nongang offenses. However, the focus of this chapter is the gang intervention program, and the sources of intra- and interorganizational conflict that were inherent in the program design.

During the late 1970s, Los Angeles County stood as the epitome of gang violence increases reported nationwide (Miller, 1982). From 1978 to 1980,

AUTHOR'S NOTE: This research was supported by Grant #81-IJ-CX-0072 from the National Institute of Justice, U. S. Department of Justice. Points of view or opinions expressed in this chapter are those of the authors and do not necessarily represent the official position or policies of the U. S. Department of Justice. We would like to thank Margaret Gordon for helpful comments on earlier versions of this chapter.

gang-related homicides increased 75% to a reported total of 351 in 1980. The local government responded by mounting a major deterrent effort. The Community Youth Gang Services Project (YGS) was funded in early 1981 as part of a coordinated multiagency task force to reduce gang violence.[1]

The program is distinctive in a number of ways. It is the only major component of the countywide task force that is not administered by criminal justice agents. The director of the project is an independent contractor with the county and city to provide gang mediation services. Modeled after the widely touted Crisis Intervention Network program in Philadelphia, YGS emphasizes a heavily deterrence-oriented approach and thereby strikes a contrast to earlier intervention programs common to the 1960s.

Between the mid-1950s and about 1970, gang intervention programs throughout the country were variations on the value transformation model. Most major urban centers in the 1960s were committed to this model, which emerged from the Chicago Area Projects (Kobrin, 1959) and the operations of the New York City Youth Board (NYCYB, 1960). The basic element was the assignment of "detached workers" to established, traditional gangs to transform their structure and value systems into more acceptable forms. There were often other components stressing community connections—schools, jobs, tutoring, recreation, parent clubs—and the detached worker was charged with liaison efforts and attaching his gang members to these alternative opportunities. Theoretical reliance tended to be placed on the tenets of differential association theory (Sutherland, 1955) and opportunity structure theory (Cloward and Ohlin, 1960).

Three major evaluations were carried out on detached worker projects, in Boston, Chicago, and Los Angeles (see Klein, 1971, for an overview of all these; also Klein, 1969; Miller 1962; Carney et al., 1969). The findings were remarkably uniform; projects that successfully engaged gang members' interests and successfully brought to bear a host of alternative opportunities nevertheless failed to have an ameliorative effect on deviant behavior. In fact, the evidence suggests that however inadvertently, the projects had the effect of perpetuating or even increasing gang cohesiveness and increasing the level of gang delinquency.

Very little new research on gang behavior has taken place. Exceptions include Miller (1982), Moore (1978), and a useful summary by Schubert and Richardson (1976). No useful evaluations have appeared. However, the time gap between 1970 and the present has reflected a major reorientation in gang programming from the transformation model to the deterrence model. Reasons for this are not hard to find. The level of gang violence has escalated, along with the availability of firearms (Miller, 1982). While Los Angeles has been the most severely affected city, reports from other cities and from cities previously free from serious gang violence usually substantiate this escalation pattern.

In addition to the increased gang activity is the increased national concern with rising violence in general, accompanied by the "neoconservative" mood of many leaders in the criminal justice and political arenas. If community leaders have come to understand that gangs cannot be readily eliminated, they have *not* settled for the increased violence that gangs are now producing. Calls for crackdowns and punitive responses are common.

The epitome of the deterrence model is the Crisis Intervention Network (CIN) in Philadelphia, and now its translation to the Los Angeles setting. The basic elements of the deterrence model are the provision of heightened street visibility and surveillance by project staff, focus on geographical area rather than specific gang, attention to violence rather than general delinquency, and intergang mediation efforts. Other elements may also be involved—parent and community councils, special liaisons with probation and police officials—but the essence of the matter is the reactivation of visible community controls and the rapid response to violent and crisis events.

To those familiar with gang intervention, there can be no mistaking the difference in the two models. The transformation model fostered social group work in the streets with empathic and sympathetic orientations toward gang members as well as an acceptance of gang misbehavior as far less of a problem than the alienating response of community residents and officials. By contrast, the deterrence model eschews an interest in minor gang predations and concentrates on the major ones, especially homicide. The worker is, in essence, part of a dramatically energized community control mechanism, a "firefighter" with a more balanced eye on the consequences as well as the causes of gang violence. Success is measured first in violence reduction, not in group or individual change.

Fourteen teams composed of six counselors (selected for their street sense and knowledge of gangs) operate from radio-equipped cars throughout Los Angeles City and County, with concentration on areas with the highest incidence of gang conflict. In order to meet the official mandate of reducing gang homicides by 15%, the teams maintain high visibility by patrolling target areas and "hot spots," establishing rapport with gang members and making contacts with the community and law enforcement. They respond on the scene to violent incidents, but much of their activity involves follow-ups to incidents that have already occurred, with a focus on preventing retaliation.

Since it was funded in mid-1981, the program has faced major obstacles to implementation and operation, and it is to these problems we now turn. Several sources of intra- and interorganizational conflict were inherent in the program's design and are presented here not only as items of research interest but as pitfalls of which future designers of intervention programs should be aware.

One source of interorganizational conflict is indigenous, perhaps, to the deterrence model. Past research has suggested that mandated relationships evidence less cooperation than voluntary relationships (Aldrich, 1976) and that under conditions of legal mandate, conflicts that arise are extremely disruptive (Hall et al., 1978). The mandate of coordination of YGS activities with law enforcement and other justice system agencies has provoked a host of difficulties. Developing trust between police and ex-gang members is a problematic task. For example, the second director of the program[2] has experienced pressure from other members of the task force and governmental officials to expand the informant role of street workers. The director argued that building rapport and maintaining the trust of gang members was essential; any violation of this trust would render the project inoperable and he threatened to resign. Similar issues arise in interaction between street workers and members of the Probation Specialized Unit.

Exchange of information is a complementary resource that can promote interorganizational cooperation (Reid, 1964). The street workers depend on law enforcement to provide current information on gang street activity and recent violent exchanges between rival gangs. On the other hand, YGS responds to community complaints of gang harassment that police are often too busy to handle. Considerable effort has been expended to develop familiarity between project staff and the law enforcement gang specialists in their target areas. These officers have been briefed on the structure and purpose of YGS, and the staff has been cautioned regarding the hazards of interference in policing activities. Achieving the delicate balance between the two agencies on the staff level appears determined largely by individual personalities. In many cases, the rapport between agencies is firmly established and enormously successful. In a number of instances, however, YGS staff has been banned from law enforcement offices.

Friction between law enforcement and YGS could be anticipated given the differences between the two groups. Incompatability of operating philosophies contributes to interorganizational conflict (Hall et al., 1977), as does the lack of shared operational goals and complementary resources such as information and client exchange (Reid, 1964). Although the two agencies share the same objective, their methods and style are very different. These differences have been aggravated by other organizational requisites. A number of the justice system agencies felt that funding for YGS came from a pool that should have been spent within their own agencies. In fact, the issue of continuing YGS funding and the omnipresent possibility of cutting the program entirely have been sources of constant concern for YGS.

The success criterion stipulated by the YGS contract was to reduce gang-related homicides by 15% during their first year of operation. Ironically, publication of the police statistics demonstrating such a reduction further aggravated the precarious relationship between YGS and one police agency.

The incidence of gang-related homicides decreased 17% during the first program year. When interviewed by the media, the director of the program failed to acknowledge adequately (at least to the ears of the officers listening) the multiagency efforts expended. The head of this law enforcement agency reported that his officers were demoralized; the statistics and efforts were theirs, yet YGS claimed the credit. The director's attempts to repair the situation were not successful; the damage, according to some officers, was done.

The other justice system agencies were not unaware of this event, and numerous rather sarcastic references have been made in our hearing in a variety of contexts. A more recent newspaper account of gang-related violent incident decreases apportioned credit to the task force, specifying all the justice system agencies without referring to YGS at all (Los Angeles Times, August 28, 1982). A follow-up article on YGS enumerated the troubled history of this agency's tenure (Los Angeles Times, August 30, 1982).

We have enumerated several sources of interorganizational tension that to some extent appear inherent in the design of the program because of its mandate to participate in the interagency task force. Other sources of tension are apparent within the project and these also seem attributable to the design. The utilization of personnel with gang familiarity and indigenous to the community is a hallmark of YGS. Yet, a history of gang association can be counterproductive to program operation. It is considered unsafe for some staff members to enter certain target areas because of past association with rival gangs. Histories of intergang conflict also surface as problems in interactions between staff. At one point, an entire team was suspended after death threats were exchanged between team members!

Since its onset, the project has been plagued by personnel turnover through both firings and resignations. Around the time we became involved in the research, the director and assistant director were replaced. Six months later, a new assistant director was hired. The three field coordinators who supervise several teams apiece change so often that it is difficult to keep track; the street worker turnover has been nearly complete. The reasons for the high personnel turnover are numerous. The director has been accused of poor management and heavy-handed tactics. Several project employees have been arrested on various charges, and allegations of drinking and drug use have provoked a number of firings. Finally, many of the street workers have chafed under authority and under the bureaucratic requisites of working for a large organization. Changes in staff are detrimental to this project in particular because it relies heavily on contacts made on the streets. Numerous firings promote conflict within the organization and have served to undermine confidence in the project. Unhappy ex-employees have expressed criticism to the local government funders, and a number have filed official complaints, contacted lawyers, initiated suits, and "gone public" with their dissatisfaction with project operations. The result of these actions has been a fairly steady barrage of bad press for YGS.

Many of the intraorganizational conflicts that have been described could have been anticipated given the qualifications and characteristics of the staff population. These problems would likely have arisen regardless of the intervention model utilized. The interorganizational conflicts, however, seem more attributable to the current model. More than two decades ago, Miller (1958) wrote about interinstitutional conflict as a major impediment to delinquency prevention; successful execution of the old transformation model of intervention may depend on cooperation between different agencies, and these interactions were common among task force administrators. However, the organizational conflict observed in the Los Angeles situation derives from the *mandated* interaction between line YGS staff and police officers and is therefore attributed as fallout from the deterrence model.

What can we say so far? "The more things change, the more they remain the same." Large gang intervention programs tend to become highly conflict-ridden. They tend to become politicized. They aim for results generally beyond their reach. As this chapter was being drafted, with the potential for conflict as we have described it, further conflicts and disruptions were to be expected.

Events have since validated the analysis. Conflicts between the YGS director and the head of one law enforcement gang unit peaked when the latter sought out the members of one street team and spoke with them regarding their feelings about the director. This then provoked a heated response from the YGS director, who complained to a county supervisor about the interagency intrusion. This episode and the director's method of responding to it resulted in his taking a month's administrative leave and ultimately leaving the program. As of this writing, the program has a third director newly installed and the program's two-year funding approaches termination within a few months. Re-funding is considered to be doubtful.

Hall and his colleagues (1977) have suggested that conflict indirectly contributes to interagency coordination through an ongoing process of conflict resolution. It is ironic that the major operational goal of YGS is conflict resolution (between gang members) and yet the failure to resolve interagency conflict may lead to the program's demise, regardless of purported evidence concerning achievement of stated program goals. Once again, research evaluation is transformed into researcher documentation.

NOTES

1. Other principal participants have been the Los Angeles Police Department, the Los Angeles County Sheriff's Department, the County Probation Department's Specialized Gang Supervision

Program, and "Operation Hardcore," a vertical prosecution unit of the District Attorney's Office with a gang prosecution mandate. See Quicker (1982) for a description of these programs.

2. The original director was fired early in the program, the victim, in our view, of an interagency power play and of his own failure to respond in a measured, noncombative manner.

REFERENCES

ALDRICH, H. (1976) "Resource dependence and interorganizational relations: local employment service offices and social services sector organization." Administration and Society 7: 419-450.

CARNEY, F. J., H. W. MATTICK, and J. D. CALLAWAY (1969) Action on the Streets: A Handbook for Inner City Youth Work. New York: Association Press.

CLOWARD, R. A. and L. OHLIN (1960) Delinquency and Opportunity: A Theory of Delinquent Gangs. New York: The Free Press.

HALL, R. H., J. P. CLARK, P. C. GIORDANO, P. V. JOHNSON, and M. VAN ROEKEL (1978) "Interorganizational coordination in the delivery of human services," pp. 293-322 in L. Karpik (ed.) Organizations and Environment: Theory, Issues and Reality. Beverly Hills, CA: Sage.

———— (1977) "Patterns of interorganizational relationship." Administrative Science Quarterly 22: 457-474.

KLEIN, M. W. (1971) Street Gangs and Street Workers. Englewood Cliffs, NJ: Prentice-Hall.

———— (1969) "Gang cohesiveness, delinquency, and a street-work program." Journal of Research in Crime and Delinquency 6: 135-166.

KOBRIN, S. (1959) "The Chicago Area Project—a twenty-five year assessment." The Annals of the American Academy of Political and Social Science 322: 1-29.

MILLER, W. B. (1982) Crime by Youth Gangs and Groups in the United States. Washington, DC: National Institute for Juvenile Justice and Delinquency Prevention. (draft)

———— (1962) "The imact of a 'total community' delinquency control project." Social Problems 10: 168-191.

———— (1958) "Interinstitutional conflict as a major impediment to delinquency prevention." Human Organization 17: 20-23.

MOORE, J. W. (1978) Homeboys: Gangs, Drugs, and Prison in the Barrios of Los Angeles. Philadelphia: Temple University Press.

New York City Youth Board (1960) Reaching the Fighting Gang. New York: Author.

QUICKER, J. C. (1982) "The Los Angeles war on youth gangs: will justice be administered?" Presented at the annual meeting of the Academy of Criminal Justice Sciences, Lousiville, Kentucky.

REID, W. (1964) "Interagency coordination in delinquency prevention and control." Social Science Review 38: 418-28.

SCHUBERT, J. G. and L. O. RICHARDSON (1976) Youth Gangs: A Current Perspective. Washington, DC: Law Enforcement Assistance Administration. (mime.)

SUTHERLAND, E. H. (1955) Principles of Criminology. Philadelphia: Lippincott.

ABOUT THE AUTHORS

TIMOTHY E. CAPLINGER earned the M.S.W. in social work from the University of Michigan School of Social Work. Currently he is a doctoral student at the George Warren Brown School of Social Work, Washingron University, St. Louis. His research interests concern antisocial behavior and the mental health of children and youths. His publications include articles concerning antisocial behavior and co-authorship of *The St. Louis Conundrum: The Effective Treatment of Antisocial Youths* (Prentice-Hall, 1983).

WILLIAM S. DAVIDSON II received his Ph.D. in 1976 from the University of Illinois at Urbana-Champaign. He is Professor of Psychology and Chair of the Ecological Graduate Training Program at Michigan State University. His research interests include crime and delinquency, community psychology, and dissemination of social programs. Davidson is co-author (with A. Goldstein, E. Carr, and P.Wehr) of *In Response to Aggression* and (with J.R. Koch, R.G. Lewis, and M.D. Wresinski) *Model Evaluation Strategies in Criminal Justice.*

JEFFREY FAGAN, Ph.D., is a Principal of URSA Institute. He is the Principal Investigator of the Violent Juvenile Offender Research and Development Program, a federally funded initiative testing treatment intervention models for violent delinquents. His previous research includes domestic violence, juvenile parole decision-making, and violent delinquency during the transition from adolescence to adulthood. Dr. Fagan also has ongoing research interests in public policy, drug abuse, and community development approaches to delinquency prevention. He received his doctorate in civil engineering from SUNY-Buffalo in 1975.

RONALD A. FELDMAN earned his Ph.D. in sociology and in social work from the University of Michigan. He is currently Professor of Social Work and Director of the Center for Adolescent Mental Health at Washington University,

St. Louis. His current research includes a three-year field experiment concerning the prevention of mental illness in children and youths. He has published numerous articles concerning antisocial behavior, group influence and group work intervention, adolescent mental health, and professional training of social workers. His books include *Contemporary Approaches to Group Treatment* (Jossey-Bass, 1975) and *The St. Louis Conundrum: The Effective Treatment of Antisocial Youths* (Prentice-Hall, 1983).

KAREN V. HANSEN is a research associate at the URSA Institute in San Francisco. She is currently working on a national Violent Juvenile Offender Research Development Program. Her research interests include juvenile delinquency, family violence, and women and work.

MICHAEL JANG is Senior Research Associate at the URSA Institute. His research interests include criminal justice system evaluation, group treatment homes for adolescents, and community treatment programs for juvenile delinquents. He has been the program chairman for Project New Pride Replication, a treatment program for serious offenders in San Francisco.

MALCOLM W. KLEIN (Ph. D., Boston University, 1961) is Professor and Chair of the Sociology Department, and Senior Research Associate in the Social Science Research Institute, University of Southern California. His active research currently includes diversion, deinstitutionalization, gang delinquency, and early sanctioning of juvenile offenders. His latest major publication is the *Handbook of Criminal Justice Evaluation* (Sage, 1980), co-edited with Katherine S. Teilmann. Forthcoming are *DSO: Comunity Treatment of Minor Offenders* (with Solmon Kobrin) and *Western Systems of Juvenile Justice*.

JAMES R. KLUEGEL is Associate Professor of Sociology at the University of Illinois at Urbana-Champaign. He has published research on the determinants of juvenile court dispositions and on criminal victimization in several major journals. He is currently involved in research on public beliefs about crime and criminality.

CHARLES H. LOGAN (Ph. D., Indiana University, 1971) is Associate Professor of Sociology at the University of Connecticut. He has published articles on evaluation research and deterrence in the *Journal of Criminal Law, Criminology and Police Science, Law and Society Review, and Social Forces.* He is currently doing research on the jury system.

JOAN McDERMOTT is Assistant Professor of Criminal Justice in the Department of Sociology and Anthropology at Seton Hall University. She received her Ph. D. in criminal justice in 1979 from the State Universtiy of New York at Albany. Her interests include the victimization of youths, juvenile delinquency, juvenile justice, and women as victims and offenders.

CHERYL L. MAXSON is a doctoral candidate in sociology and a research assistant at the Social Science Research Institute, University of Southern Calilfornia. She currently directs a research project on gang violence. Prior areas of research include the prediction of legislative modification, assessment of legislative implementation, and juvenile diversion programs.

MERRY MORASH received her Ph. D. in 1978 from the Institute of Criminal Justice and Criminology at the University of Maryland. She is now an assistant professor in the School of Criminal Justice at Michigan State University. She has published *Juvenile Delinquency: Concepts and Control* with Robert Trojanowica, *Implementing Criminal Justice Policies*, and numerous articles. Her publications and research focus on policy analysis, women in the criminal justice system, and juvenile delinquency.

SHARLA P. RAUSCH (Ph. D., University of Connecticut, 1982) a senior partner at Social Policy Research, has just completed her dissertation on "Perceptions of Sanctions, Informal Controls, and Deterrence: A Longitudinal Analysis." Her interests center on social control theory and delinquency. She has published in *Journal of Research in Crime and Delinquency.*

JOHN A. SAUL received his M.A. in ecological psychology from Michigan State University in 1981. He was a research assistant with MSU Adolescent Diversion Project from 1979 through 1981. His prior publications and papers have dealt with youth advocacy in the juvenile court, measuring change in community interventions, and energy conservation program evaluation. He is currently an evaluation analyst with the Michigan Energy Administration, where he is researching the effectiveness of utility energy conservation programs.